# ACCESS YOUR ONLINE RESOURCES

*7 Dimensions of Highly Effective SENCOs* is accompanied by an online booklet of printable resources, designed to ensure this resource best supports your professional needs.

Go to https://resourcecentre.routledge.com/speechmark and click on the cover of this book.

Answer the question prompt using your copy of the book to gain access to the online content.

# 7 DIMENSIONS OF HIGHLY EFFECTIVE SENCOS

This accessible and empowering book helps SENCOs and their line managers to define what leadership of SEND means in practice and how SENCOs can continue to grow and develop in their role.

Combatting the lack of clarity, identity and agency often associated with the position, the book defines career aspirations for future and practising SENCOs. It examines the SEND leader trajectory from initial teacher training to advanced leadership using an evidence-based model and practical tools to measure strengths and further areas for development. The book is divided into two parts, first examining the SENCO role before focusing on seven 'habits' needed to maximise effectiveness.

Chapters include:

- Original research broken down into an accessible and impactful guidance reference for use in schools.
- Spaces for reflection to help readers build a sense of identity, agency and power.
- Top tips to support recruitment and retention, as well as unpacking the role to consider pressure points, strengths and challenges from a task-based perspective.
- A wealth of case studies, vignettes and quotes outlining what working in and with the SLT entails, as well as an exploration into the difference between SEND strategy and long-term planning.
- An analysis of seven key skills for the SENCO/SEND leader role, with suggestions for developing these to grow and succeed.

With advice on leveraging agency and managing power to improve standards of delivery and drive positive change, this book is essential reading for both experienced and trainee SENCOs looking to build a successful career, as well as teachers transitioning to the role. It is a useful tool for leaders with little experience in SEND who are line-managing SENCOs and will also be valuable reading for headteachers and MAT leaders.

**Dr Anita Devi** is still a part-time SENCO. As a former Senior Leader, local authority SEND Advisory Teacher, SEND School Improvement Advisor and Healthwatch Trustee, Anita brings a wealth of perspectives to the table. In 2017, she was awarded the prestigious international Influential Educational Leaders Award for her SEND Pipeline strategy. In her substantive role, Anita is currently a Changemaker Education Consultant, researcher and author, as well as Founding CEO of #TeamADL, leading several innovative solutions such as #Provision Reviews for SEND MAT Due Diligence and #365send.

# 7 DIMENSIONS OF HIGHLY EFFECTIVE SENCOS

Defining a Career Trajectory for SEND Leaders

Dr Anita Devi

LONDON AND NEW YORK

Designed cover image: Getty Images

First published 2025

by Routledge
4 Park Square, Milton Park, Abingdon, Oxon OX14 4RN

and by Routledge
605 Third Avenue, New York, NY 10158

*Routledge is an imprint of the Taylor & Francis Group, an informa business*
© 2025 Anita Devi

The right of Anita Devi to be identified as author of this work has been asserted in accordance with sections 77 and 78 of the Copyright, Designs and Patents Act 1988.

All rights reserved. No part of this book may be reprinted or reproduced or utilised in any form or by any electronic, mechanical, or other means, now known or hereafter invented, including photocopying and recording, or in any information storage or retrieval system, without permission in writing from the publishers.

*Trademark notice*: Product or corporate names may be trademarks or registered trademarks, and are used only for identification and explanation without intent to infringe.

*British Library Cataloguing-in-Publication Data*
A catalogue record for this book is available from the British Library

ISBN: 9781032814933 (hbk)
ISBN: 9781032814926 (pbk)
ISBN: 9781003500131 (ebk)

DOI: 10.4324/9781003500131

Typeset in Optima
by Deanta Global Publishing Services, Chennai, India

Access the Support Material: https://resourcecentre.routledge.com/speechmark

**Dedicated to SENCOs around the world**

*those I have met, and*

*those I have yet to meet.*

I am grateful for all that you do and the dedication with which you do it. If this book can go a small way to making your working lives easier, then the seven years of research and writing this book have been totally worth it.

Some parts of this book may surprise you; other parts will stretch you. But most of all I hope this book inspires you to be the best version of yourself. This doesn't mean working harder, but smarter, connecting heads, hearts and hands in a more impactful way.

Ultimately it is the children, young people and their families we serve that will benefit.

At the time of writing this book, I was part-time back in school being a SENCO myself!!!

So, I have written this for you, as one with you.

# Contents

Acknowledgements — xi
Acronyms — xiii
Icons — xv

Introduction — 1

## PART 1

1. What 'being' a SENCO means? — 8
2. Is being a SENCO for me? — 15
3. What to look for in potential SENCOs? — 22
4. What to consider when transitioning from teacher to SENCO? — 31
5. How to anchor SENCO identity whilst doing the day-to-day job? — 40
6. What does it mean to leverage agency in order to improve standards of delivery? — 46
7. How to define and manage power in order to drive change? — 55

## PART 2

Introduction of the SEND Leadership Model — 63

8. Dimension 1: Specialist knowledge — 68
9. Dimension 2: Leadership skills — 81
10. Dimension 3: Critical thinking skills — 94
11. Dimension 4: Interpersonal skills — 105
12. Dimension 5: Strategic decision-making skills — 118
13. Dimension 6: Professional skills — 130
14. Dimension 7: Structured approach to SENCO Continuous Professional Development (CPD) — 138

# CONTENTS

**PART 3**

Final coda 155

References 159
Index 171

# Acknowledgements

The year this book was first published marks 40 years since I had the call to work in education. Over this time period family, friends and colleagues have all shaped my life and my professional perspective. Through their kindness, encouragement and challenge, I would like to think I am more courageous, more compassionate and a bit wiser. I am grateful and loved. Y'shua, you will always be my first love, my confidant and my strength (HPiTP).

This book would not have been possible without the input of my supervisor to my PhD at Lancaster University – Dr Melis Cin. Her feedback, signposting and questioning have played a significant part in shaping my thinking and my final thesis. I'm proud of what has emerged, and I sincerely hope it makes a difference. But equally (if not more), the journey of studying under her supervision has been an absolute joy and privilege. *Teşekkür ederim* – for those not familiar with this phrase, it means 'I thank you' in Turkish.

I'd also like to thank the team at Routledge Publishing for trusting my ideas. In particular, heartfelt hugs to Clare Ashworth and Molly Kavanagh. It was a joy to work with you on *Journeying to the Heart of SENCO Wellbeing* in 2022. This experience has extended this joy exponentially. What will our next joint venture be?

My gratitude extends also to Stephanie Derbyshire and the team at Deanta for their patience in typesetting and editing. Their feedback was invaluable.

Many reviewers vetted the initial book proposal. I truly appreciate their feedback, especially Michelle Storer of Hays Education, who kindly looked over some of the HR aspects of the additional materials that accompany this book.

Whilst I may have written this book, it came together through a team of people. That is the foundation of SEND Leadership – teams.

# Acronyms

| | |
|---|---|
| APL | Accredited prior learning |
| BC | Before Christ [Time reference] |
| BELMAS | The British Educational Leadership, Management and Administration Society |
| CPD | Continuous professional development |
| CYP | Children and young people |
| D | Disability |
| DfE | Department for Education |
| EFA | Exploratory factor analysis |
| EHCP | Education Health and Care Plan |
| FRaIM | Frameworks for an Integrated Methodology (Plowright, 2011) |
| GB | Governing body |
| HEIs | Higher education institutions |
| INSET | In-service training days |
| ITT | Initial teaching training |
| JD | Job description |
| LA | Local authority |
| MAT | Multi-academy trust |
| MKO | More knowledgeable other |
| nasen | National Association of Special Educational Needs |
| NASENCO | National Award for Special Educational Needs Co-ordination |
| NPQ | National Professional Qualification |
| PD | Professional development |
| PE | Physical education |
| PGCE | Postgraduate Certificate of Education |
| PhD | Doctorate of Philosophy |
| PS | Person specification |
| QTS | Qualified teacher status |
| RA | Reasonable adjustments |
| RIG | Research and interest group |
| RUFDATA | Reason, use, focus, data, audience, timescale and agency (Saunders, 2000) [evaluation approach] |
| SCM | Success case method |
| SDG | Sustainable Development Goals (United Nations) |
| SEN | Special educational needs |
| SENCO | Special Educational Needs Co-ordinator |
| SEND | Special educational needs and disability |
| SEND CoP 2015 | The SEND Code of Practice 2015 (DfE) |
| SEND7 | Seven stakeholder groups (children and families, support staff, teaching staff, SLT, those responsible for governance, external agencies and the SENCO) (Devi & Bowers, 2022) |

## ACRONYMS

| | |
|---|---|
| SEND8 | SEND7 plus MAT Central Team |
| SLIM | SEND Leader Integrated Model (Devi, 2022) |
| SLT | Senior leadership team |
| TSL | Thought self-leadership |
| ZPD | Zones of Proximal Development (Vygotsky, 1896–1934) |

# Icons

Action task:

In your shoes:

Additional materials:

Question:

Further reading:

Case study:

Top tips:

New:

Further training:

Myth busting:

Reminder:

Legislation:

PART 1

# Introduction

This book is designed to help you define your story and your career trajectory as a Special Educational Needs Coordinator (SENCO). So, I thought I would begin with my story. Not that you should copy this or that it was ideal, but hopefully it will highlight how we can stay true to a calling, whilst navigating the twists and turns of the sector. My story demonstrates the lens through which I see things, as well as my 360-degree perspective of the system. Throughout the book, I have included quotes from SENCOs, thereby giving you a broader perspective of different views.

At any moment in time, we are the summation of all our experiences to date and these moments define our lens of observation. So let me begin by sharing my story:

*I started teaching in my local community at the age of 12. Pretty young right! I was involved in teaching other children the mother tongue of my parents' birthplace. By 14, I knew teaching and education was my vocation, my calling. By now I had transitioned from language teaching to 'Character Education' and the inculcation of human values as a core curriculum component. By 18, I was writing teacher training manuals for voluntary teachers like myself across the country and abroad. Not the most conventional childhood into adulthood experience. But in those six years, I had found my why – 'the joy of learning'. This isn't about those 'light bulb moments' some teachers talk about, this was about the transformative growth of individuals for a greater good. Yes indeed, I was at that age where being a visionary was the norm. Ironically, my own experience of receiving education or formal learning encounters from others wasn't all that brilliant. Like most, I had a few excellent teachers, and the others weren't bad per se, I just wasn't experiencing 'the joy of learning'. I was increasing my knowledge and skill base, but I wasn't always experiencing the development of me as a person. I did often wonder, did my teachers enjoy teaching us? Did they care, or was it just a job? Those who did inspire us were passionate about something. Primary teachers I found enjoyed and thrived on child development. Secondary teachers were passionate about their subject area. This observation I have confirmed many times when working with colleagues in schools and colleges as an adult. One of my most vivid experiences in sixth form was from my work experience module. I ended up working in a special school for severe and complex needs. I learnt so much, and although these students couldn't speak or move, I knew they knew the joy of learning!*

*Many moons later, I entered the classroom as a teacher. So, who did I teach and what did I teach? Early years was my starting point. This was an amazing season of seeing four-year-olds manipulate four-digit numbers and learn the foundations of life. One year, a selective mute girl in my class was the first to see a caterpillar emerge from its cocoon as a butterfly ... she started speaking at that moment. Oh, the joy! Sadly, the curriculum we were delivering was something the government was not keen on in the mainstream. This was my first interaction with seeing the politics of education. I moved into secondary education and taught pupils for whom English was an additional language (EAL) as well as mathematics. I loved my subject areas, but I loved learning more! We would undertake eight-week assessment cycles of the students' progress. As a fairly new teacher professionally, I was keen for the students to give me feedback on my teaching. How could I do better and how could I harness the learner voice for my professional development? This was in an era when pupil voice wasn't necessarily the norm. I placed an open book at the front of the class and asked students to give me feedback on my teaching. It was all anonymous, and to my colleagues' surprise, many students took the time to give me honest feedback. Many shared what helped and others said what could be better. I was open to both. One Year 11 boy shared, 'Miss, when I sit fidgeting with my pen, you think I am not learning, but that's how I learn. The motion of the pen mirrors the motion of my thoughts'. What an insight! I was truly grateful because what he was telling me was that, unknowingly, I had defined the evidence of learning through the expectation of certain behaviours. The next day, I zoned out from the pen fidgeting and I started to see how he was learning.*

*I enjoyed my work, and I enjoyed working in the department. But there was a defining turning point. One of our students had gone missing. Safeguarding was a very selective 'need to know' process then, with a single point of contact, as opposed to the team approach we now adopt. This girl had told each of us teachers different pieces of the puzzle about her intentions, but it was only when she went missing that we put it together. This incident frustrated me immensely. School systems were part of the problem, but I began to question how well (on a two-week timetable system) I really knew my students. I discovered the secondary model didn't give me space to know and understand students in a way that would maximise their learning.*

*Two other different incidents followed that led me to finally move into the middle school and primary sector. The first was quirky but made me reflect on how well I communicated. I was overseeing the work experience of students. I arranged for one student to work in a framing shop from 10 am to 3 pm each day. On the first day, he didn't show up until 2:50 pm (10 to 3). The second was through teaching Year 7s. I noticed some of the basic skills needed for classroom learning and routines were missing. This really impressed on me the need for early intervention.*

*As a primary teacher, I was seen to have a classroom ethos that enabled all children to demonstrate progress. One eight-year-old came to my class; prior to this, he had been expelled from five other schools. He stayed in my class for two years, as I taught the year group as they moved up. I learnt that sometimes exclusion just becomes about passing the perceived problems on, rather than supporting the learner. Something I stood up against many years later as a SENCO.*

*Throughout my journey, 'the joy of learning' has remained my anchor, my why and my intent. What challenged me time and time again was when children were not accessing learning, it was/is my responsibility to do something about it. This could include changing how I talk, present materials, structure the work, construct groups and so on. As teachers, we do not take an oath like doctors, but I deeply believe we are required to ensure all children placed before us make progress. That's our responsibility. I noticed many in my classes couldn't access the learning and experience this joy. It made me question myself over and over until I found solutions that worked.*

*Working as a SENCO, senior leader and class teacher was an experience I relished. There were many challenges, and you will hear of some throughout this book. I never imagined myself leaving the classroom, but local political situations led me to becoming a SEND advisory teacher and later a SEND advisor. Over the years, I have trained many SENCOs through their formal L7 induction qualification (called NASENCO at the time of writing) and for one institution being an external examiner. I have also developed SENCOs through questioning, challenging, coaching, mentoring, imparting, bespoke training, writing, speaking and modelling what I believe to be effective leadership of special educational needs and disability (SEND).*

*In England, national policy changed. First in 2008 with the SENCO Regulations and then in 2011–2018 with The Children and Families Act 2014. I was part of the process of shaping, constructing and enabling. I had high hopes for our system, but sadly what eventually was enshrined in law complicated the system. The 2008 act meant every school had to have a SENCO; however, the cost was a compromise on the quality of the appointment. The 2014 Act brought in a greater variance of localised processes that technically aligned to one nationally agreed approach. But they didn't. The NASENCO changed from being about the 'co-ordinator' (i.e. the person) to 'co-ordination' (i.e. what they did). There were gaps in policy and in some areas too much specificity. Added to this was the problem of interpretation.*

*We needed to construct a different way of leading. In 2017, I embarked on an education and social justice PhD at the University of Lancaster. I would not consider myself to be a pure academic in the sense of someone who likes to debate possibilities and theorise. I am a change strategist and policy-maker. I consider all the possibilities and then having made an informed choice, I define a trajectory for growth and change. The four-year study programme offered was absolutely incredible and I am grateful to all my tutors. None of the academic part came easy to me but what was clear to my tutors was that I knew my field and I wanted to use research to improve a very complex system.*

*On completion, I chose not to publish academic papers, but to write this book and design two accredited courses. There may be more in the future. But for now, I want what I have learnt and discovered to help those in the system break the strongholds that prohibit leaders from being effective and children and young people from receiving the support they need. I do not claim to have all the answers, but this is a start. My hope is that those who read this will go further than I have.*

### In your shoes:

Take a blank sheet of paper and chalk out your journey. The non-negotiable threads, transferable skills and the twists and turns. Highlight moments of 'perseverance'. Consider, how this affects your current lens.

Let me now tell you about my research that forms the backbone of this book:

The research was conducted over two years of field work (June 2018 to May 2020). There was an initial evaluation study using the success case method (SCM). This involved a sample of ten experienced SENCOs in England and deep conversations to consider and examine whether the National SENCO Award (NASENCO) was fit for purpose.

In 2008, the SENCO Regulations Act made the NASENCO a mandatory 'induction' qualification for any new appointees that had to be completed within three years of appointment. The same Act also stipulated that SENCOS had to have achieved 'qualified teacher status' (QTS) prior to appointment. In subsequent chapters, I will address the pros and cons of this induction training. It should also be noted that at the time of writing, the NASENCO was in the process of being changed from September 2024 into the National Professional Qualification (NPQ) SENCO. Since my main research beyond the initial evaluation study did not focus on this induction training (regardless of title and structure), the questions I raised and the conclusions I came to remain valid.

The SCM evaluation approach was a seven-dimensional structure called RUFDATA, which stands for reason, use, focus, data, audience, timescale and agency (Saunders, 2000). The evaluation study was conducted in two parts, adopting two methodologies: an online survey and semi-structured telephone interviews. The online survey consisted of 18 questions, six of which were open-ended for qualitative responses and 12 of which were quantitative, and of these, 83% were closed-choice responses. The semi-structured interview (conducted after the online survey) was divided into five main sections that focused on experience, context, motivation, NASENCO experience and the SENCO role.

The evaluation study highlighted the need to focus my study on what happens prior to appointment and post-induction training.

## Research design

The main research was conducted in three qualitative research phases based on the extended FraIM design (Plowright, 2011).

**Phase 1:** These were face-to-face discussion forums known as a research and interest group (RIG). This was funded by the British Educational Leadership, Management and Administration Society (BELMAS). There were no conflicts of interest associated with receiving this funding and undertaking the research.

The first discussion group unpacked in detail Regulation 50 (Children and Families Act, 2014). This Regulation details the job description of the SENCO role in legislation. More about this in Chapter 1. The second discussion focused on teacher identity and was led by an external academic. SENCO identity was the focus of the third discussion and was also utilised to ensure that as a previous SENCO, I was not bringing my own bias to the research. All three forums took place within an academic year. In the third session, SENCOs reported 12 identity tensions of undertaking the role, these resonate with Hughes (2002) and can be summarised in Table 0.1.

*Table 0.1* SENCO Identity challenges in the 'day-to-day' as reported by SENCOs at a BELMAS RIG Meeting (2019)

| | | | | |
|---|---|---|---|---|
| 1 | Perception | ⟷ | Reality | What the position entails? |
| 2 | Self | ⟷ | Others | How to enable others? |
| 3 | Management | ⟷ | Leadership | Operational or strategic? |
| 4 | Quick wins | ⟷ | Long-term strategy | What does impact look like? |
| 5 | School (demographics) | ⟷ | Senior leaders (with limited knowledge) | Who shapes the role? |
| 6 | Isolation | ⟷ | Team | Who is involved and responsible? |
| 7 | Day-to-day | ⟷ | Driving change | What to focus on? |
| 8 | Learner needs | ⟷ | Whole school change? | What does success look like? |
| 9 | Completing 'tasks' | ⟷ | Agency to be innovative | What's expected? |
| 10 | Internal values and desirable working ethos | ⟷ | External and diverse stakeholders | Which values drive the agenda? |
| 11 | Popularity pleasing | ⟷ | Doing what's right | What criteria define decisions? |
| 12 | Reflective teacher/many roles | ⟷ | Criticality of focused leadership | How is diverse data synthesised? |

### Action task:

Make some time to reflect on these tensions and questions. Which can you relate to?

**Phase 2:** An online questionnaire was used to seek the views of 110 SENCOs from across the country in operating in different phases between November 2019 and March 2020. This overlapped with schools going into lockdown due to the pandemic. An online short video (less than two minutes in length) was used to introduce the purpose of the research and snowball sampling (Bryman, 2016) was used to engage participants. The questionnaire consisted of 32 questions divided into six sections. Settings from across 11 regions in England took part covering Early Years to Key Stage 5.

**Phase 3:** The original plan had been to use Photovoice (Pearson & Ralph, 2007) to explore the identity, agency and power of SENCOs. However, with an international pandemic changing school dynamics, this evolved into 24 in-depth semi-structured interviews. These were conducted online. From the questionnaires (Phase 2), only 10% expressed a desire to be involved further in interviews. The remaining 90% of participants engaged in the interviews were acquired through snowball sampling. Cohen and Arieli (2011) argue that in conflict environments, when individuals experience marginalisation, outsiders increase trust and engagement through snowball sampling.

My role in the interviews was not just to 'mine' for information, but to 'travel' alongside, meeting people and experiencing different landscapes (Kvale, 1996). The interviews were divided into four sections:

1. Background information pertaining to the individual.
2. Setting specifics regarding the individual in situ.
3. The continuous professional development opportunities and career pathway of the individual in situ (actual and aspirational).
4. The individual's perception of leadership based on Clapp-Smith et al. (2019).

Six visual prompts were also used as part of the interview, as well as the online whiteboard for freedom of expression. The modal number of years of SENCOS participating in the interviews, since qualifying was six, with lower and upper limits ranging between one and nine years, respectively.

On completion of my PhD, it was not my intent to write academic papers, but instead produce guidance and tools for practitioners to use and develop in themselves.

This book is a part of the practical application of my research; as such, it is split into two sections. The first asks questions and Part 2 focuses on the solution output from my research. Other online tools and accredited training courses have been developed alongside. Contact www.teamadl.uk for more details.

## How to use this book?

Initially, read all the way through. Part 1 provides a framework and Part 2 focuses on practical application. You need both. In time, it's possible that Part 2 will be your focus as you continue to dip in and out of Part 1.

The book is a combination of my considered views and the underpinning research. I have endeavoured to balance both so you as the reader can benefit from experience and evidence.

PART 1

# 1 | What 'being' a SENCO means?

The role of the SENCO in England requires a practitioner to bring together complex national legislation with dimensions of policy and practice plus local dynamics. At the time of writing, the national government is trying to bring about some national consensus through, for example, standardised templates for statutory processes. However, this is not an overnight change, and it may take years for this to be fully actualised.

In this chapter, I deconstruct Regulation 50 of the Children and Families Act 2014 to look at the role of the SENCO under the microscope. The Special Educational Needs and Disability (SEND) Regulations are classified as a Primary Statutory Instrument. They state explicitly what is required, by law. The SEND Code of Practice 2015 (SEND CoP 2015 hereafter), which many use for knowing the 'how to', is a Secondary Statutory Instrument. Many distinguish these two instruments by stating the Regulations imply what 'must' be done and the Code defines what 'should' be done. There is a mismatch between the two and so for the purposes of my research I focused on Regulation 50, i.e. what must be done.

Regulation 50 is entitled 'Appropriate authority functions and duties relating to the SENCO'.

The wording below has been adapted slightly from the legislative language to simply list the duties, without losing the functional meaning or the order. The list below was used as a visual stimulus during the in-depth interviews (Phase 3). During the interviews, care and consideration were given to the format for those with dyslexia and/or other learning needs.

1. Informing parents/carers as soon as possible of pupils considered to have a special educational need.
2. Identifying a pupil's special educational need and co-ordinating provision to support.
3. Monitoring the effectiveness of the special provision made.
4. Securing relevant services for the pupil (in-house and externally).
5. Maintaining and updating records of a pupil's special educational need and provision put in place.

6. Liaising with parents/carers and providing regular information regarding their child's need and the provision made.
7. Ensuring all the right information is passed on when a pupil transfers to another school/institution.
8. Promoting inclusion in the school community, as well as access to the school's curriculum, facilities and extracurricular activities.
9. Selecting, supervising and training learning support assistants who work with pupils with special educational needs
10. Advising teachers about differentiated teaching methods appropriate for individual pupils with special educational needs.
11. Contributing to training for teachers to assist them in carrying out identification, implementing provision, monitoring, record keeping, parent liaison and promoting inclusion.
12. Preparing and reviewing the SEN Information Report, which is published in the public domain.

As already stated, the order of these 12 'authority functions' has not been changed. I would argue the order is incoherent in determining the role of the SENCO and I will address this later in the chapter.

 **In your shoes:**

Depending on your role, similar and different questions may arise about these 12 functions listed. Table 1.1 asks some of these, you may have others you wish to add. Reference to SEND 7 is about the different stakeholders and this is taken from 'Journeying to the Heart of SENCO Wellbeing' (Devi & Bowers, 2022, p. 36).

None of this is easy, and yet, we have over time assumed that a single induction qualification can solve all these issues. Is it a leadership role or a management role? Should the SENCO be on SLT? The discussion around position, power, authority and agency is addressed in Chapter 7.

What we do need to consider though is how we reframe these 12 'authority functions' into a functional framework. You can also download additional support materials as outlined at the beginning of this book.

**Additional materials:**

- The job description of a SENCO.
- A suggested timeline for delivery.

Table 1.1 Possible questions arising from the 'authority functions' of a SENCO (Regulation 50)

| SEND 7 | Possible questions ... add your own too. |
|---|---|
| 1. Children and families | • How often will I be informed and how?<br>• How will need be identified and how often will support change or evolve?<br>• What progress is required to determine effectiveness?<br>• What records are kept of us and for how long?<br>• How regularly will I be updated?<br>• Will ALL details be passed on? What if important information is missed out?<br>• What does inclusion feel like, how will I know? |
| 2. Support staff | • How will I be selected?<br>• What will supervision look like?<br>• What training will I receive and how often? |
| 3. Teaching staff | • What's my role in all of this?<br>• How do I access 'advice'?<br>• What ongoing training do I need, and will this match what I need? |
| 4. Senior Leadership Team (SLT) | • How do we best line manage and support a SENCO to do this?<br>• What data should we be looking at?<br>• How do we know things are going well or if there is a problem, especially in situations when the SENCO doesn't know?<br>• How much training time and resources should we be making available?<br>• How does this affect other priorities? |
| 5. Those responsible for governance | • What should we be expecting and monitoring in terms of information? And how often?<br>• How do we support and challenge?<br>• Although there is delegated responsibility, does the ultimate responsibility rest with us? |
| 6. External agencies | • What information should we expect during the commissioning of services? What if we are not given the full picture?<br>• What if our advice is not followed through?<br>• What if we do not have the time or capacity to support the setting? |
| 7. SENCO | • When am I meant to do each function and how much time to allocate?<br>• How do I know?<br>• What does 'authority function' really mean in practice? |

## Redefining the SENCO role, whilst maintaining the essence of Regulation 50

To redefine the SENCO role, we must zoom out to zoom in. The bigger picture embraces different dynamics as highlighted in Figure 1.1.

This bigger picture defines relational constructs. Obviously, any one of the four elements could change, but knowing how they link together helps increase 'agility' when change comes. This relational approach also ensures that the SENCO role is perceived as both leadership **and** management. It is not an either/or scenario. The sweet spot is obviously in the middle. However, the main three components are continuously changing. Making it a dynamic environment to work in.

 Question:

Prior to training and appointment, how many SENCOs are informed of the dynamic nature of the role? Why is this significant? Being a SENCO requires a certain level of resilience. Research by Dobson and Douglas (2020b) concludes that four interest factors predominantly determine the application of new SENCOs. These will be addressed in Chapter 2.

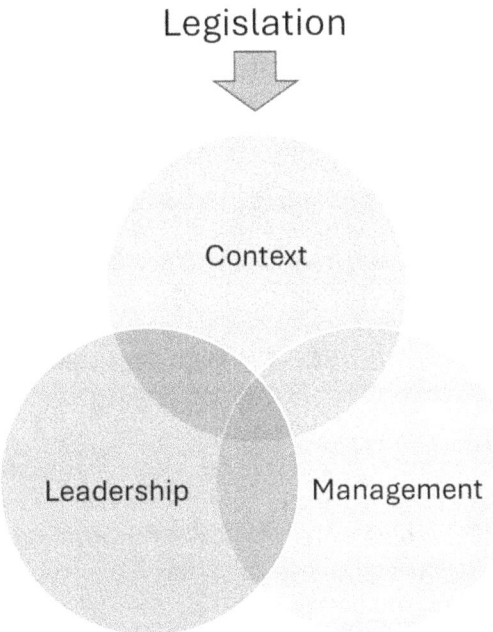

*Figure 1.1* Understanding the interaction between national legislation, local setting/context and the SENCO role (both leadership and management)

*Table 1.2* Six areas of SENCO leadership and management (covering Regulation 50)

|  | Theme | Regulation 50 |
|---|---|---|
| Leadership | Whole setting – developing and delivering change/improvement | #8 Promoting inclusion in the school community, as well as access to the school's curriculum, facilities and extracurricular activities<br>#10 Advising teachers about differentiated teaching methods appropriate for individual pupils with special educational needs<br>#11 Contributing to training for teachers to assist them in carrying out identification, implementing provision, monitoring, record keeping, parent liaison and promoting inclusion |
|  | Leading others | #9 Selecting, supervising and training learning support assistants who work with pupils with special educational needs |
|  | Accountability | #3 Monitoring the effectiveness of any special provision made<br>#12 Preparing and reviewing the SEN Information Report, which is published in the public domain |
| Management | SEND knowledge and experience | #2 Identifying a pupil's special educational need and co-ordinating provision to support<br>#4 Securing relevant services for the pupil (in-house and externally) |
|  | Relational connections | #1 Informing parents/carers as soon as possible of pupils considered to have a special educational need<br>#6 Liaising with parents/carers and providing regular information regarding their child's need and the provision made |
|  | Administrative efficiency | #5 Maintaining and updating records of a pupil's special educational need and provision put in place<br>#7 Ensuring all the right information is passed on when a pupil transfers to another school/institution |

Without a doubt, the role of the SENCO is complex. Redefinition of the SENCO role can occur through three processes:

1) **Reductionism** – reducing the scope, volume or descriptor of the role. However, this does little to impact change at the ground level and often leads to more confusion.
2) **Simplicity this side of complexity** – basically, this involves listing 'activity tasks' under each 'authority function'. Once again, this becomes a prescriptive approach. O'Toole (1993) argues that 'Managers who clamour for how-to instructions are by definition, stuck on the near side of complexity' (p. 12). In other words, the how-to lists are only successful if XYZ conditions exist and those conditions remain steady and stable. Figure 1.1 highlights how impossible that is. So, at best, the 'how-to' or 'should' scenarios create wisdom based on a false premise.

WHAT 'BEING' A SENCO MEANS?

3) **Simplicity the 'other' side of complexity** – research, dialogue and experience combine to deepen understanding that isn't about 'perfect conditions' for operating but 'pattern seeking' using The Gestalt Principles, or Laws of Perception, to form a clearer and coherent model. Wulf (2020) argues that The Gestalt Principles help to configure or structure perception as a physical whole. This gives rise to better organisation and spacing and can influence timing.

Adopting the third process above, I would argue the 12 'authority functions' of the SENCO, stipulated in law, could be simplified to six core areas, covering three areas in leadership and three areas in management. These are shown in Table 1.2, where each 'authority function' in law is shown via a hashtag (#).

The summary of this can be seen in Figure 1.2, which extends the dynamic environment mentioned in Figure 1.1. The person specification (PS) to accompany this is discussed in Chapter 2.

**Action task:**

Reflect on the table groupings in Table 1.2. How does this align with your role or perception of the SENCO role? Do you operate from a balance of leadership and management or mostly in management-mode?

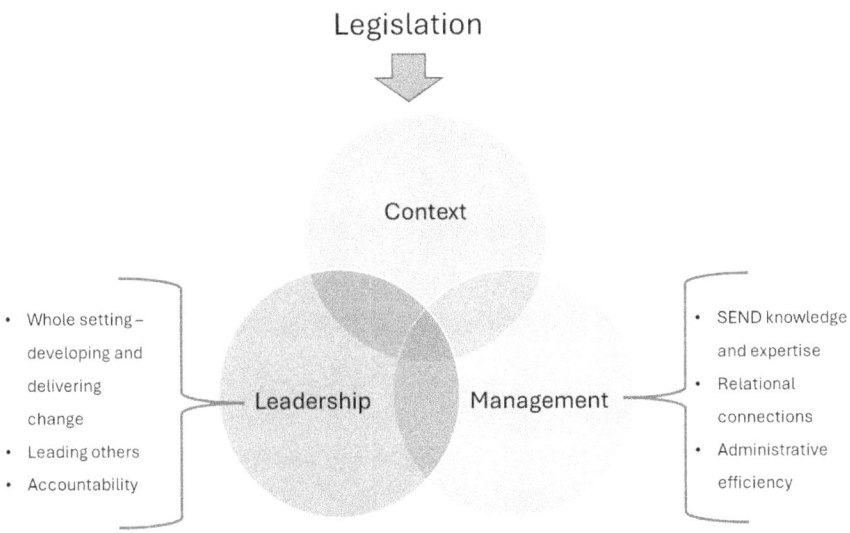

*Figure 1.2* The interaction between national legislation, local setting/context and the SENCO role (both leadership and management) in terms of six areas of 'authority functions' as defined by Regulation 50 (DfE, 2014)

**Action task:**

Consider how your understanding of the SENCO role has shifted as a result of reading this chapter. What did you know before and what do you know now?

## Summary

This chapter has deconstructed the SENCO role in terms of the legislative requirements and a functional model for leading and managing.

Chapter 2 considers whether the SENCO is suited for all or some with defined skills and attributes.

PART 1

# 2 | Is being a SENCO for me?

*People tell others who they are, but more importantly they tell themselves, and then try to act as though they are who they say they are.*

– Holland et al., 1998, p. 1

**Being a SENCO isn't for everyone!**

This may sound like a pretty harsh statement to make. But it is true. In Chapter 1, the job description (JD) of the SENCO role was deconstructed into six key areas. In Part 2, I will demonstrate how these map onto the SEND Leader Integrated Model (SLIM) (Devi, 2022), which helps define a career trajectory of growth. The application of SLIM is unpacked in more detail in Part 2 of this book.

As a reminder, what I proposed in Chapter 1 is the SENCO JD (based originally on Regulation 50) and is defined as a combination of leadership and management (Table 2.1).

In this chapter, I want to explore voices from the field about what the role actually entails. The broader aim of this chapter is to work towards a person description (PS). The JD and PS work in tandem, and anyone recruiting a SENCO would need to consider what aspects are the non-negotiables and what aspects of the role can be learnt. By and large, the right attitude is not something that can be learnt, however, skills and knowledge can be acquired. Sometimes I have seen SENCOs appointed for skills and knowledge and little, if any, weighting is given to leadership and management attitude. In subsequent chapters, we will extend our thinking to explore teachers applying to be SENCOs, what factors influence the transition into being a SENCO, how professional identity is impacted and why a single induction qualification isn't enough.

*Table 2.1* Six areas of SENCO leadership and management (covering Regulation 50)

| Leadership | Management |
|---|---|
| • Whole school setting – developing and delivering change/improvement<br>• Leading others<br>• Accountability | • SEND knowledge and experience<br>• Relational connections<br>• Administrative efficiency |

DOI: 10.4324/9781003500131-3

The constructs 'ability' and 'capability' are both nouns, with their difference positioned in pragmatics. Ability can be regarded as a qualitative marker of skills and attributes. These usually sit on a continuum, with the prospect of growth, be that a higher level, deeper understanding and/or broader application. Ability is three-dimensional. Capability tends to be more of an either/or scenario. There is no continuum. They either can or they can't. So, what bridges ability and capability is capacity, i.e. human potential. In theory, any able-bodied person has the capacity to ride a unicycle, yet not all have the ability or capability. The same is true of the SENCO role. In a classroom, a teacher may demonstrate a high ability in supporting the needs of vulnerable learners, but they do not have the capability to lead others and translate those personal skills into a whole-setting vision for growth under difficult circumstances.

Difficult circumstances here imply challenging situations. The growth of SEND pupils continues to increase year on year and so needs will always outstrip resources. In effect, leading special educational needs and disability (SEND) is about holding something that will continually be in tension and continually open to change. This professional lifestyle, therefore, isn't for everyone.

Additional materials:

- Person specification of a SENCO based on SLIM Leadership Model (Devi, 2022).
- Reflective narrative journal for SENCOs based on SLIM Leadership Model (Devi, 2022).

## Leadership

### Whole school setting – developing and delivering change

This requires someone who has a vision, can articulate it and then communicate it to a variety of stakeholders (SEND7, Devi & Bowers, 2022). So, in effect, this involves three distinct abilities that are learnt skills, however, underpinning a vision is a set of core values about teaching and learning and leadership. *This bilingualism in educational parlance (teaching and learning + leadership) is a capability.*

*Abilities*

i. Defining a vision: This is harder than most people realise. A vision is not a long-term plan of sequential steps, nor is it a strategic process for driving change. Both of these are required once a vision has been defined. A clearly articulated vision transports people into the future, in the present tense, as if they were already there. What would they see and experience? How can they be part of it?

ii. Articulating a vision means using simple, jargon-free language for others to form the same picture in their hearts and minds. Not only must other team members see it, but they must also believe in a pathway to achieve it.
iii. Communicating a vision involves persuasion. Aristotle (384 BC–322 BC) connected the dots between 'trust' and 'persuasion'. In doing so, he defined a rhetoric that is based on three strong pillars – ethos (ethical arguments), pathos (emotional buy-in) and logos (logical disposition). For persuasion to be effective, thereby increasing trust, all three need to be in play. Trust is often quoted as the missing factor in the SEND system (Lamb, 2009).

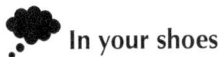 **In your shoes:**

Think back to the last presentation you heard or gave on SEND or Inclusion. Was there a balance of ethos, pathos and logos? If affirmative, how did this provoke you into action and/or increase trust? If not, what was missing and why?

A further capability dimension to consider is the SENCO's relationship with change. Some people thrive on change, others avoid it. As John Maxwell often states, 'Change is inevitable, but growth is optional'. Change will happen, and as leaders, you can go through the motions without growing. However, to embrace change and grow from it is the hallmark of an effective leader. It serves to create a learning culture and ethos for others in the team.

### *Leading others*

First and foremost, leadership is about building teams. In *Journeying to the Heart of SENCO Wellbeing* (2022), Jenny and I describe at length who is on the SENCO's team and how they need to consider different stakeholders.

Here I would add three additional ability points of consideration:

i. The commitment level of a SENCO to create teams beyond a formal department or group of support staff is vital for whole-setting ownership. People contribute when they feel part of something. A newly appointed SENCO can often want to gain credibility by demonstrating their own knowledge and expertise at the expense of truly building a wider team.
ii. How well does your SENCO switch between leading and being led? Effective leaders develop other leaders because they recognise that leadership isn't about post or position, but influence. In effect, they can understand the need to be both confident and humble at the same time.
iii. Bringing people together from different roles with different ideas and lenses will inevitably result in different opinions and possibly conflict. So, an attitude where differing opinions is seen as healthy plus the skill to navigate conflict becomes vital.

Many SENCOs enter the role with a personal desire 'to make a difference'. However, they struggle when two or more people have different views on the best way forward.

## *Accountability*

Much of what the SENCO has to do on a day-to-day basis is follow through on processes within defined systems and a setting-based structure. Any process involves three key points – preparation, delivery or execution and review for growth. Each point requires a different dimension of accountability expressed through professional curiosity, awareness, empathy plus reflective and reflexive thinking.

i. **Preparation** embraces stillness for defining forethought. Understanding a range of possible outcomes and mitigating risk from any foreseen negative outcomes. This could also involve seeking the views of trusted and experienced others, not just through social media but also through established relationships.
ii. **Delivery and execution** are completed when agility and flexibility are built into the culture and process. We can plan and consider all the possible options, however, it is often only when the process is live in context and under the current circumstances that the reality of what's possible, what's not and what may obstruct unexpectedly comes into view. Reacting to these changing dynamics can produce further negative consequences or problems. However, learning to respond within the right time frame becomes an important skill of leadership.
iii. **Review for growth** occurs, I believe, at three levels. There are ongoing everyday reflections plus termly reflexivity to draw out key patterns and trends and finally an annual end-of-year accountability narrative to governors and parents. The three build on each other and the interaction produces a system that is open to transformation and growth.

## Management

### *SEND knowledge and expertise*

In my research, this was the area in which SENCOs invested most of their professional time. Many believing that if they 'showed' they knew more, this would earn them the gravitas of a respected leader. However, what was also uncovered was that both professional development (PD) and continuous professional development (CPD) opportunities are chosen on three dimensions: cost, time and availability. So, in effect, there is no strategic connection to personal growth or leadership development.

At the core, three main areas support SENCO development, as well as the transition from teacher status to SENCO status. These include:

i. A sound understanding of effective pedagogical practice in the classroom. This comes from both experience, but also keeping up to date with new research and evidence-based approaches.

ii. A growing understanding of child and young person development. Key milestones and challenges. These map onto the four broad areas of need mentioned in SENDCoP 2015.
iii. An understanding of SEND policy (national law and local practice). It is against this backdrop that their knowledge of pedagogy and child/young person development should be placed at the centre, as a reference point.

When recruiting a new SENCO who is transitioning from teacher to SENCO, I would expect them to be fairly knowledgeable about an effective classroom and how to articulate it to others, plus show an understanding of child/young person development.

*Relational connections*

There needs to be an intentionality in building new relationships that incorporates three core approaches to communication:

i. When people are nervous, or in unfamiliar environments of change, the tendency can be to talk more. Figure 1.1 (Chapter 1) highlights three dynamic aspects of the role. However, a key skill for SENCOs is to listen and assimilate diverse views.
ii. As stated previously, effective leaders build teams, and for the SENCO, this is about building teams where there is a culture to accept/give support as well as challenge each other. Without challenge, teams can stagnate and become stuck in 'this is how we have always done it'.
iii. A third dimension is motivation. Teams that feel they 'are in the loop' and/or have the information they need tend to be more proactive and open to new ideas.

 **In your shoes:**

Do team members see SEND Support across the setting as a piece of Swiss cheese, wholesome but with gaping holes that only the SENCO can fill, or do they see a solid block of cheese, giving them clarity of the overall connectivity? *(For those of you who don't do cheese, a similar metaphor could be applied to a knitted garment – lots of gaping holes or an interconnected structure?)*

*Administrative efficiency*

This is the final dimension of management, which in many cases becomes the focus of the SENCO role. Yet no SENCO applies to the role 'to do the paperwork'.

> *I would like my career progression to be a coach of other teachers, supporting them to develop themselves so they can be the expert in their classroom. I think SENCOs spend too much time on complex paperwork and less time providing support to other staff about how to help their children.*
>
> – SENCO Q15 (Devi, 2022)

# 7 DIMENSIONS OF HIGHLY EFFECTIVE SENCOS

What three dimensions define administrative efficiency?

i. The ability to think in processes and not just tasks. Tasks can become unending to-do lists that are often placed on them. However, when a SENCO thinks about a process, there is scope to involve others and improve efficiency.
ii. The ability to reflect, take on feedback and commit to improvement or better ways of working.
iii. Recognition that accountability (at different levels) is part of the role and communicating efficiency is important to increase confidence and trust in the system. Some would call this empathetic administration, i.e. an awareness of the impact on others.

## Why do teachers apply to become SENCOs?

Dobson and Douglas (2020a) identify the different drivers that motivate a teacher to apply for a SENCO role. Depending on whether the determinants are microsystems (i.e. direct experiences), mesosystems (i.e. aspirational for involvement and change), exosystems (i.e. driving change) or macrosystems (i.e. shaping the wider system) (Anderson et al., 2014; Dobson & Douglas, 2020a), a SENCO's vision, values and approach can be impacted. It should be noted that the data for the Dobson and Douglas study (2020a) was collected from participants early on whilst undertaking the NASENCO induction course.

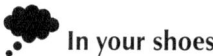 In your shoes:

How many SENCOs are asked the motivation question during an interview and how many interviewees then classify the response according to the Dobson and Douglas (2020a) research? Surely this impacts whether the needs of the context (Chapter 1, Figure 1.1) are being met.

## What should we expect from SENCOs?

Based on the SEND Leaders Integrated Model (SLIM) (Devi, 2022), the SENCO role embraces six critical dimensions. These are:

1. Specialist knowledge
2. Leadership skills
3. Critical thinking skills
4. Interpersonal skills
5. Strategic decision-making skills
6. Professional skills

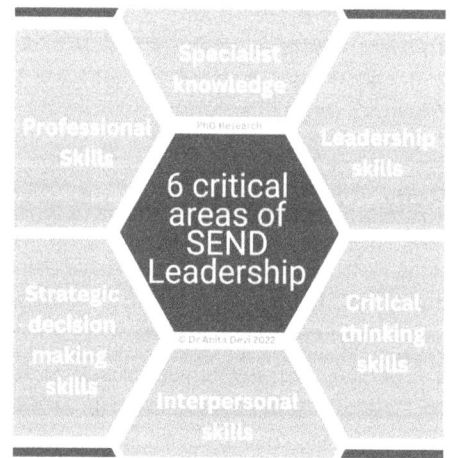

The seventh dimension is a planned CPD pathway for growth (see dimension 7 in Part 2).

# IS BEING A SENCO FOR ME?

Table 2.2 Reflective task covering six dimensions of SLIM (Devi, 2022)

| Dimension of SEND leadership | What this means to me | What would this look like in my setting? What behaviours would I see? |
|---|---|---|
| 1 Specialist knowledge | | |
| 2 Leadership skills | | |
| 3 Critical thinking skills | | |
| 4 Interpersonal skills | | |
| 5 Strategic decision-making skills | | |
| 6 Professional skills | | |

 **Action task:**

Before reading further (especially Part 2), use Table 2.2 to record your thoughts about each dimension. Could this model be applied both at the setting and multi-academy trust (MAT) level?

## Summary

This chapter covered in more depth the leadership and management role of a SENCO.

Chapter 3 reflects on the dynamics of SENCO identity, agency and power. These three were the cornerstone of my original research.

PART 1

# 3 | What to look for in potential SENCOs?

**Picture the scenario**

School ABC needs to recruit a SENCO. Four candidates apply (see Figure 3.1). Three have never been a SENCO before and one of these is an internal applicant. The fourth is an experienced SENCO who has completed the induction qualification (NASENCO or NPQ SENCO).

As part of the SLT selection panel, how do you decide? The first three would have to complete the induction qualification within three years (England, SENCO Regulations, 2008; Children & Families Act, 2014). Assuming this is completed – does completion of the qualification level the playing field?

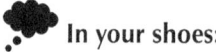 **In your shoes:**

What other factors will affect the effectiveness of their leadership?

As part of my research (Devi, 2022), I invested time looking at the transition from teacher to SENCO. This, in fact, is a maturation process from pedagogical agency to leadership agency.

**What are identity and agency and why do they matter?**

Most SENCOs seek to influence others in the SEND7 (power), as it constitutes the connector between perceived self-construct (identity) and action (agency). Sherman and Teemant (2021) extensively discuss the triad between identity, agency and power for teacher action. I have applied this relational construct to the role of the SENCO.

Being a teacher is foundational to being a SENCO. Teachers make countless decisions daily (Havik & Westergård, 2020). They are agents of change (Van der Heijden et al., 2018), influencing and contributing to students' engagement (Olivier et al., 2020), learning (Agathangelou et al., 2016), relationships (Quin, 2017), personal growth and development (Rhoades et al., 2009; Farrow et al., 2020; Thorpe et al., 2020), as well as long-term prospects (Chetty et al., 2014). Education is a complex process of

# WHAT TO LOOK FOR IN POTENTIAL SENCOS?

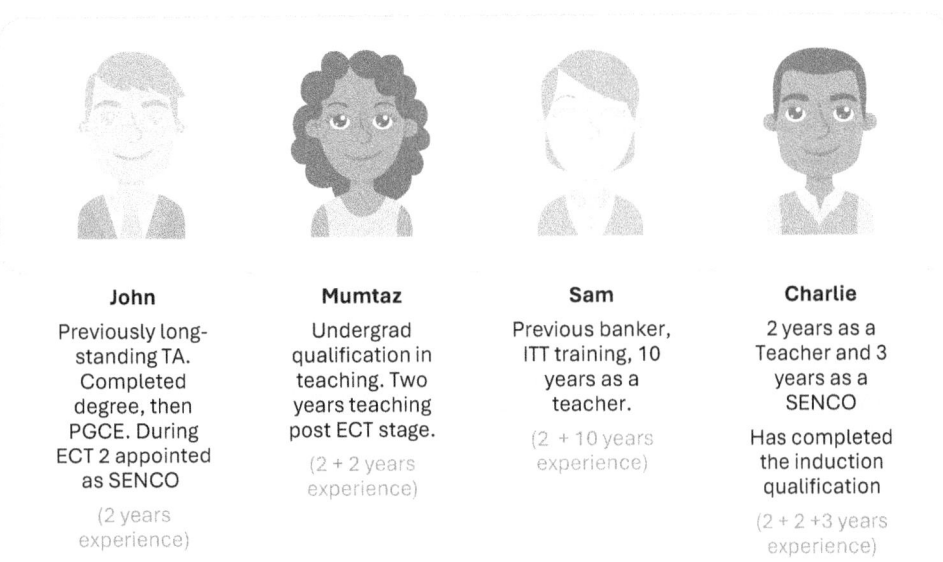

*Figure 3.1* Possible four candidates for the post of SENCO at School ABC

content-driven interactions (Bower, 2020) and experiences (Wilkinson & Penney, 2014; Robinson, 2016). The teacher and their belief systems play a key role in facilitating the process of inclusion (Williams-Brown & Hodkinson, 2021). In effect, teacher identity (a self-construct), teacher agency (teacher action) and teacher power (degree of influence) are critical to the discourse, especially given that 68% of SENCOs are also class teachers (Dobson, 2019).

## *Identity*

Trent (2011) proposes that the layering process of teacher identity construction can take up to four years to establish authorisation, rationalisation, moral evaluation and accurate discernment of myths. Defining 'teacher identity' is problematic (Beauchamp & Thomas, 2009). The construct is dynamic and multi-dimensional and shifts as teachers progress through teacher education and beyond the initial four construction years proposed by Trent (2011). Beauchamp and Thomas (2009) also highlight further shifts throughout career progression associated with wider interactions within schools and the community outside the school.

In reviewing the research, Coe et al. (2014) identified six factors that determine great teaching in terms of improved student outcomes: namely, pedagogical content knowledge, quality of instruction, classroom climate, classroom management, teacher beliefs on learning and professional behaviours. These six pillars of what makes great teaching

(Coe et al., 2014) therefore form the basis of appointing an effective SENCO and the role they must perform. In contrast, Kearns (2005) uses metaphorical phenomenology to classify the SENCO identity as one that is an arbiter, a rescuer, an auditor, a collaborator and an expert. Hallett (2021) presents a case for the SENCO role to be seen in terms of processes and systems. Legislation defines teacher identity in terms of Standards (DfE, 2012) and the SENCO in terms of tasks (Regulation 50, Children & Families Act, 2014).

As part of my research (Devi, 2022), I undertook a thematic approach to Regulation 50 (SEND Regs, 2014). These define the 'authority functions' of a SENCO (see Chapter 1).

Five core themes emerged, with an additional outlier, which is relevant to the discussion on wider leadership.

- **Theme 1**: Relationships and liaison with parents and carers (points 1 and 6).
- **Theme 2**: Identification, co-ordinating and monitoring of provision (points 2 and 3).
- **Theme 3**: Record keeping, information management and reporting (points 4, 5, 7 and 12).
- **Theme 4**: Training support staff and teachers (points 9 and 11).
- **Theme 5**: Advising teachers (point 10).
- **Outlier**: Promoting inclusion across the school (point 8).

The process of advising teachers (theme 5) has been distinguished from training (theme 4) as different leadership dynamics are involved in the process and potentially a different level of agency.

*Agency*

Discussing shared phenomena using duoethnography methodology, Banegas and Gerlach (2021) put forward the case to suggest a teacher's sense of social justice and responsibility is critical in determining their agency and identity. Teacher and SENCO agency can be perceived as the capacity to influence, make choices and take a position in a way that positively affects their practice (Eteläpelto et al., 2015). Critical to enhancing agency is the pursuit of professional development (Beauchamp & Thomas, 2009). This will be discussed in Part 2.

Some argue SENCO agency should be provided through automatic access to a senior leadership position. Look back at Figure 3.1. With such varying backgrounds and teaching experience, should senior leadership membership be a blanket acquisition on appointment? Focusing on research, I pick up this discussion further in Chapter 7.

What is relevant for recruitment is understanding that SENCO professional agency emerges from identity (Clarke, 2009) and 'identity work' is an intentional series of actions that give rise to beliefs around professional, cultural, political and individual values.

## Maturation and metamorphosis process

Identity can consist of both stable and unstable identities (Day et al., 2006; Day, 2007; Sammons et al., 2007) within a wider evolving process of identity formation (Clarke, 2009) and adaptive practices to educational reform.

There are six key points in the determined trajectory of a SENCO (A to F) as shown in Figure 3.2. It could be argued A to C form the foundation of an early career, where the individual brings a core part of themselves and their background to their training and starts to assimilate teacher identity and agency. Different training routes (Carter, 2015) and backgrounds often have an impact on how quickly teacher identity and agency are adopted. Qualified teacher status (QTS) in England can be achieved through both undergraduate study and postgraduate qualifications. Dobson (2019), looking at national workforce datasets of SENCOs in 2017, deduced that 48.3% qualified as teachers through a postgraduate route. Thus, reflecting a first degree in a specialist area plus an increased number of years of life experience and postgraduate studies, compared with an undergraduate. Brown and Doveston (2014) reflect on how a lack of postgraduate prior training impacts those undertaking the NASENCO in terms of developing higher-order critical thinking and writing skills required at Level 7 and for accurate identification when in the role. In other words, for about 50% of the population undertaking the NASENCO, providers need to place a greater emphasis on academic skills, whilst at the same time meeting the expectations of a professional competence-based award. This may shift further still, as the proposed NPQ SENCO (start date September 2024 at the time of writing) is significantly different. The time gap can add significantly to the teacher development process, particularly if, during that time, the individual (point A in Figure 3.2) has worked in a different industry and/or has had a family and thereby experienced child development as a parent (Quintrell & Maguire, 2000; Smith et al., 2013; Rushton, 2014; Murtagh, 2017).

The inclusion and SEND policy arena in England is predicated on the social justice platform of using person-centred approaches (Docherty, 2019). This is about providing opportunities to improve services for those who use them (Boswell & Woods, 2021) by those who use them. Using qualitative research methods over five years from two university-based teacher education providers, Essex et al. (2019) adopt this approach to examine pre-service science teachers' views of inclusion in all their complexity. They sought to determine reflective practice (application of what has been learnt) and critical reflexive practice (assumptions and implications of what has been learnt) in relation to the widening definition of inclusion, which also politically included the government's Prevent Strategy and British Values curriculum (DfE, 2014). Out of the 13 questions asked during interviews, five are pertinent to this discussion (Essex et al., 2019, p. 6):

1. What teaching strategies for inclusion have you learnt about during the PGCE [*teacher training*]?
2. In what ways has the university-based work prepared you for inclusive teaching?

# 7 DIMENSIONS OF HIGHLY EFFECTIVE SENCOS

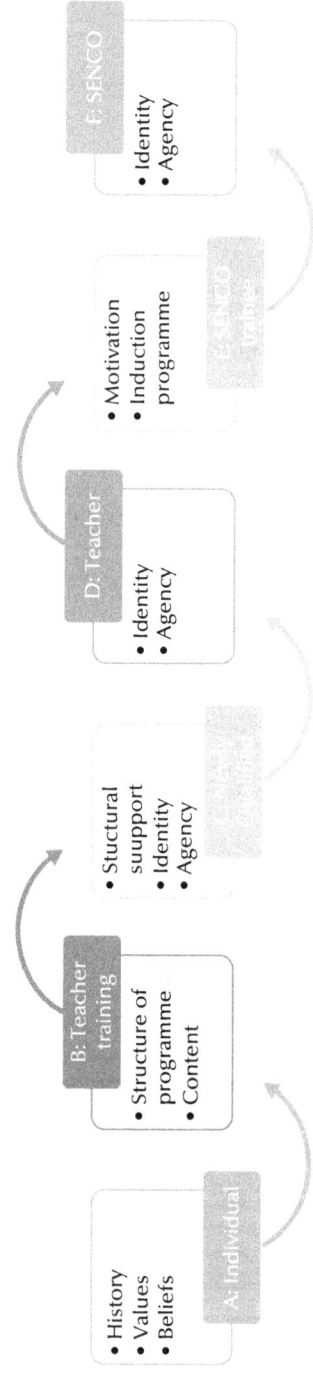

Figure 3.2 The determined projective of a SENCO (Devi, 2022)

3. Were there any aspects of inclusion taught in university that appeared to be at odds with what you saw in school?
4. Are there any groups at risk of underachievement which you don't feel confident to teach effectively yet?
5. What do you understand by 'inclusion in teaching'? Which specific groups of learners (if any) do you think stand to benefit from an inclusive approach to teaching and learning?

 Question:

How useful would variations of these questions be for SENCO interviews, focusing not only on their own views but also the enablement of colleagues, which is part of the SENCO role (see Chapter 2)?

## Adaptions

1. What teaching strategies for inclusion have you used successfully in your classroom and would recommend to others?
2. In what ways has your background, values and teaching practice work prepared you for inclusive teaching?
3. Were there any aspects of inclusion you implemented in your classroom that appeared to be at odds with the wider school?
4. Are there any groups at risk of underachievement which you don't feel confident to teach effectively yet?
5. What do you understand by 'inclusion in teaching'? Which specific groups of learners (if any) do you think stand to benefit from an inclusive approach to teaching and learning?

The potential conflict (individual vs institution values) in practicum is particularly drawn out in question 2 (DeLuca, 2012; Gavish, 2017). Using an interpretive critical approach, Essex et al. (2019) found that whilst pre-service teachers regard inclusion as a positive and abstract construct, their experiential evidence focused on ability models and 'othering' (Jones et al., 2020). As such, the trainee teachers struggled to distinguish learners who were educationally vulnerable or demonstrated low ability from those with special educational needs. Other student teachers commented that whilst at university they had had sessions on different types of learners, translating this to the classroom with multiple needs simultaneously was challenging, thus concluding, in one instance, that 'inclusion shouldn't have to include everybody' (Group B, student teacher A). Based on these tensions and perceptions, practical strategies to implement inclusion were minimised to single-dimension differentiation (top, middle and bottom), but without any clarity on what differentiation means in terms of the learning environment. Elsewhere, I have shown there are 18 approaches to differentiation (Devi, 2016). There was also evidence of reflective practice; however, reflexive understanding was less prevalent. Given that most students shared a deficit-based notion of inclusion, Essex et al. (2019) conclude that a key barrier in teacher education is the 'teach to the standards' and 'teach to the test' thinking of pre-service students. The root thread of this resting is in the policy context of the wider sector.

Point D is an opportunity to embed practice and consider long-term career options. Assuming the practitioner chooses to become a SENCO and is successful in their application, then there is a transition zone to consider motivation (see Chapter 2) plus initial training, which I call an induction programme or qualification. At this point, in theory, they are a 'trainee SENCO', yet so many are thrust into the role as trainees 'acting' like 'experts'. Does this create imposter syndrome? Just like teaching, post-qualification, the appointed SENCO needs to embed their SENCO identity and consider further growth trajectories. It is this part, and the transitions from D to F and beyond, that the current system fails to consider, both at the point of recruitment and as part of the retention process.

Case study:

Mercy Academy has an experienced SENCO who is keen to move into a deputy head role. Sebastian, a teacher within the school, is keen to become a SENCO. The school finances are strong, and they set up a coaching programme for Sebastian to do part of the SENCO role for a year. The purpose is to see whether this is really for him. The existing SENCO works alongside him. At the end of year one, Sebastian is determined to continue, so in year two, he is given more responsibilities and embarks on the induction qualification. The existing SENCO works alongside him. In year three, Sebastian takes on the full SENCO role and the existing SENCO moves to another school as deputy head.

The case study is the ideal scenario for succession planning, but we know in reality this is not always possible. Financial pressures and sudden departures of personnel force schools to recruit and the field isn't always so varied.

Action task:

With the growth of multi-academy trusts (MATs), it is possible for a prospective SENCO to shadow a SENCO in three different settings for a day and write up their learnings as part of the recruitment process. Is this time-intensive? Absolutely, however, it could ensure the most suitable candidates, who know some aspects of the reality of the role, are recruited.

Let me draw this chapter together by suggesting three top tips for recruitment.

# WHAT TO LOOK FOR IN POTENTIAL SENCOS?

Top tips:

1) In designing the SENCO recruitment process, consider how applicants both **declare and demonstrate** their experience to date, as well as how they articulate their 'why' for choosing to be a SENCO as part of their career progression (see motivation in Chapter 2). This is relevant as SENCOs need to adapt regularly between working on their own and working with others in teams.
2) Be intentional in discovering how the candidates talk about their identity, agency and power as teachers (or SENCOs, if existing). Which leadership model does this resonate with the most? Have they considered alternative methods?
3) Focus on how potential candidates will use their SENCO identity and agency to influence others in your setting towards greater improvement. In particular, how they deal with conflict and different data pieces that may appear contradictory.

Action task:

What are your top three takeaways from this chapter and how will you use this in your setting?

1.
2.
3.

Additional materials:

- List of suggested recruitment tasks.

Further reading:

Devi, A. (2020). (Series Editor Hollis, E.) *Essential guides for early career teachers: Special educational needs and disability.* London: Critical Publishing.
Devi, A., & Jagger, S. (2025). *Neuroplasticity and neurodiversity in the classroom.* London: Critical Publishing.

Further training:

SEND in the Classroom (2022) Accredited Course on the Four Areas of Need by High Speed Training.

## Summary

This chapter considered the dynamics of transitioning from teacher identity and agency to SENCO identity and agency. Tips and strategies were also provided to support recruitment.

Chapter 4 focuses on how to execute the transition from teacher to SENCO.

PART 1

# 4 | What to consider when transitioning from teacher to SENCO?

*Apart from the national induction qualification, there has been nothing printed to date that supports the transition from teacher identity to SENCO identity. This gap creates a potential space for imposter syndrome instead of building on the strengths of previous experience. This can manifest a wide range of behaviours. This chapter unpacks the importance of managing professional identity change to counteract imposter syndrome.*

### Is promotion to a SENCO a linear trajectory?

First and foremost is the question, is appointment to SENCO 'perceived' as a promotion? Douglas and Dobson (2020a) conclude that teachers draw on a wide range of reasons for applying to become a SENCO. However, given the statutory nature of the role, in many schools in England, the role is undertaken by the headteacher, deputy headteacher or assistant headteacher. Examining data from 2017, Dobson (2019) showed that 10.6% of the SENCO population was comprised of headteachers, 12.1% deputy headteachers and 15.5% assistant headteachers. In each of these 'identities', there is a question to be asked as to which role takes precedence in terms of identity, time allocation and priority. In addition, what was the sequential order of appointment? The classroom teaching population of SENCOs was at the same time 61.8%, with 28.9% in a part-time post (Dobson, 2019). The data does not aggregate different roles with full- or part-time employment status. Therefore, it is possible for a SENCO to be full-time on site but only part-time in the role or a SENCO to be part-time on site but have no other role other than that of a SENCO.

### Why apply to be a SENCO?

A key factor in the SENCO identity discourse is the motivation or reason SENCOs apply for the role. Using exploratory factor analysis (EFA) of 32 potential reasons why a SENCO might apply for the role, Dobson and Douglas (2020b) conclude that four interest factors predominantly determine applications. These are subcategorised into outward- and inward-facing factors, as shown in Table 4.1. Outward-facing relates to a school/setting focus based on a rights agenda and on good classroom practice, whereas inward-facing revolves around professional development and experience. This reflects a dichotomy in

*Table 4.1* Four interest factors for SENCO applications (Dobson & Douglas, 2020b)

| Outward-facing | Inward-facing |
|---|---|
| • Broader inclusion agenda<br>• High-quality provision | • Educational and professional development<br>• Leadership voice and status |

role-identity between pedagogy (outward-facing) and leadership (inward-facing). The contrast was reported as statistically significant, with most of the teachers' interest being rooted in outward-facing factors. All 618 participants in the study were undertaking the NASENCO at the time of this research (Dobson & Douglas, 2020b).

In other words, is the application and subsequently the appointment based on 'bigger picture' ideals (outward-facing) or personal goals (inward-facing)? Identity and agency differ in both of these rationales based on the 'perceived' area of influence and change. It would be wrong for us to expect everyone to apply for the same reason. However, it is important to consider how the 'why' factor impacts approach and performance. Many SENCOs also report a third factor, not raised in the research by Dobson and Douglas (2020b), namely, the 'no-choice' factor. Usually comments like, 'I was asked' or 'There was no one else' take precedence in such scenarios. This is particularly true in countries like England where the role is a statutory requirement. In some cases, the quality of leadership will be compromised.

I would suggest an additional complexity that is often reported by SENCOs. This is whether they take up the post in their existing setting or move to a new place. The latter tends to bring about a quicker development of identity and agency. However, the learning curve in terms of new setting processes, personnel and gaining credibility is steep and this often slows leadership progress down. SENCOs promoted in-house already know the systems and people but often live in the shoes of their predecessor or their previous roles. This is particularly tricky if their predecessor remains in the same setting as well or if, in their previous role, they were perceived in a specific way (e.g. early career teacher).

## Two models of transition

The current modus operandi in England is that, regardless of background or motivation, anyone appointed has to have qualified teacher status (QTS) and complete the mandatory induction within three years. Beyond this, there is no defined career progression, method of appraisal or method for quality assurance.

Let me therefore suggest and critique two models of transition.

# TRANSITIONING FROM TEACHER TO SENCO

*Figure 4.1* Linear progression trajectory from teacher to SENCO (Devi, 2022)

## Model 1: Linear trajectory

In this approach, progression is seen as a discrete set of steps and then tails off after the mandatory induction qualification has been completed. This model can also be tricky, if, for example, the newly appointed SENCO decides to complete the induction qualification in their third year. Most professional roles include a probationary period. However, for the appointment of a SENCO, this is rarely seen in practice.

Theoretically, this model makes sense. However, how many SENCOs start their role from a place of pedagogical agency? Most focus on the SENCO knowledge deficit model, and so agency is eroded from the onset and an over-emphasis is placed on acquiring SEND knowledge over developing as a leader who already has sound pedagogy as a classroom practitioner.

 Case study:

Chris has joined a new school as the appointed 'new SENCO'. The school invests financially in her enrolling and attending the induction qualification. This lasts approximately 18 months. It is during this time that Chris realises the SENCO role isn't really for her. Who can she tell? What about the financial burden on the school? Would resigning have an impact on her career and would she have to move schools? The contractual aspects of a SENCO appointment are rarely given much thought, and this often creates internal conflict and misalignment for the SENCO.

Each SEND7 stakeholder also potentially carries an interpretative framework about the role of the SENCO (Smith & Broomhead, 2019) and what they expect the SENCO to do (Day, 2007 cited in Buchanan, 2015; Passy et al., 2017) in their context (Holland & Lachicotte, 2007; Reeves, 2009; Varghese et al., 2005, Douglas & Dobson, 2020b). Against this backdrop, a SENCO is therefore required to co-ordinate these diverse interpretative frameworks, whilst simultaneously trying to lead and implement legitimate and authentic actions (Sherman & Teemant, 2021) that align with their own beliefs and values. This can further serve to enhance discordant identity position beliefs and/or imposter syndrome.

It should be noted that SENCOs who are also part-time teachers often report greater productivity in their teaching commitments than as a SENCO. I would argue this is because their teaching timetable is more structured and protected than their SEND leadership time. I am not convinced protected leadership time is the solution (Curran et al., 2018). In Part 2, I put forward a case for protected CPD that is currently missing.

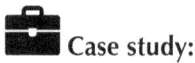 Additional materials:

- From the TeamADL eStore (https://www.teamadl.uk/e-store/) download the SENCO Time Management booklet entitled 'Take Time' (Devi, 2016) or refer to 'Journeying to the Heart of SENCO Wellbeing' (Devi & Bowers, 2022).

*Model 2: Metamorphosis approach*

Unlike the trajectory discrete approach (Figure 4.1), this model, as shown in Figure 4.2, creates space for the overlap by morphing the teacher into a teacher leader, grounding identity in leadership and then transitioning into SENCO. In relation to Figure 3.1, this would probably mean John and Mumtaz would not be considered as viable candidates until they have substantial teaching experience to become teaching leaders.

Case study:

Sarah was encouraged by her SLT to apply to be the SENCO within her own school. She opted to complete the training in her second year. In her first year, she made time to familiarise herself with the current systems in place. A coaching model with an external specialist was put in place for the first year, so Sarah had the freedom to discuss any issues she was facing without fear of losing face with her peers or leaders. During her end-of-year appraisal conversation, Sarah took the SENCO JD to the meeting to discuss which aspects were relevant and which aspects needed refining. The new version was

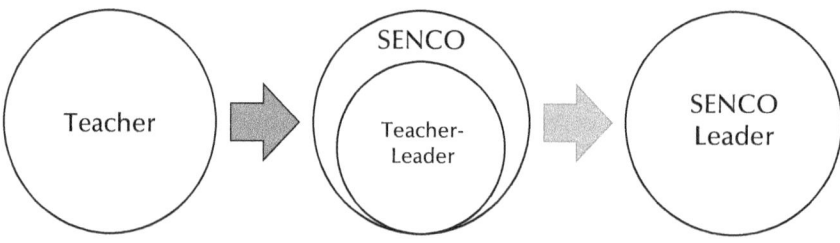

*Figure 4.2* Overlap metamorphosis model from teacher to SENCO (Devi, 2022)

then shared with the SEND Governor. This became a year-on-year practice in the school as Sarah developed in her role.

## Exceptional cases

It is usually at this point in the discourse that colleagues raise specific case studies of experienced teaching assistants who have obtained QTS and want to become SENCOs. They have considerable 'classroom' experience, and so it could be argued that they could undertake the role. I think this is a case-by-case discernment moment. The only caveat I would raise is, does the fast-track SENCO see the role as leadership or management and what influence currency will they have with teachers who have been teaching for many years? Could this potentially push the role back into being a 'specialist' role and more about doing paperwork than enabling others?

There are no easy answers. However, what is clear is further thought needs to be given to the transition from teacher to SENCO, ensuring there are opportunities for SENCOS to develop their sense of 'being, doing and enabling' (as in Figure 4.3).

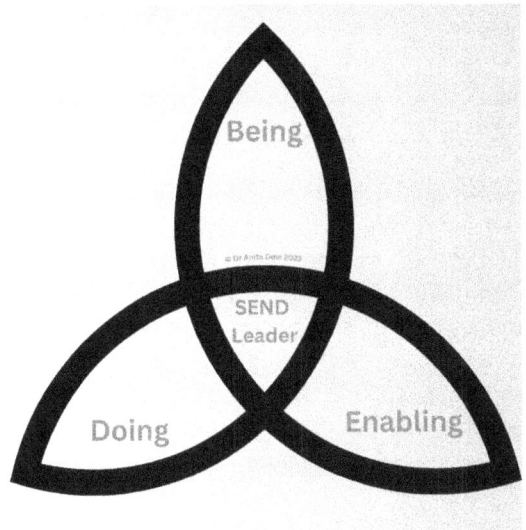

*Figure 4.3* Three dimensions of SENCO action that need to work together for SENCOs to flourish

https://www.sencoleader.pro/

 **Idea:**

What if, instead, an asset model was used as part of the SENCO's induction to record current strengths and areas of development based on SLIM (Devi, 2022)? The standard induction qualification implies everyone needs the same initial start. It is, therefore, a model of resource equality, but not necessarily identity and agency equity.

*What are your thoughts on this?*

 **Question:** Can the generic be applied to the specific?

We can see that, whilst the term 'SENCO' is a generic term used to define a role and leadership identity, what happens in practice differs from context to context. Now imagine the complexity of these diverse identities (context-driven) within a wider identity of a multi-academy trust. The result is often comparison and/or copying when, in reality, the universal strategy adopted does not apply to their context. In effect, the SENCO role embodies a national top-down framework of expectations and localised school-based interpretation and variation (Garner, 2001, Tissot, 2013) through different values and multiplicity of experiences prior to entering the role (Day et al., 2007; Rosen-Webb, 2011).

The previous induction programme (NASENCO) was defined by learning outcomes that covered professional knowledge and understanding, leading and coordinating provision plus personal and professional conduct. Over the years, several studies have examined *the **impact** of the NASENCO*, a Level 7 qualification (Griffiths & Dubsky, 2012; Brown & Doveston, 2014), or have involved candidates on the NASENCO (Tissot, 2013; Done et al., 2016a, 2016b; Clark, 2017, Dobson & Douglas, 2020a, 2020b). Using surveys (n=56 across eight local authorities), Brown and Doveston (2014) evaluated the impact of NASENCO on co-ordination and leadership, strategic management of policy and provision, teaching and learning and working in partnership with pupils, families and other professionals. Whilst they discuss the preparedness for postgraduate study, they do not consider whether the NASENCO compulsory qualification leaves SENCOs 'feeling prepared'. Likewise, Griffiths and Dubsky (2012), using the metaphor of gardening (operational duties) and landscaping (strategic leadership), try to link the impact of the NASENCO to micro and macro development. What these studies fail to consider is the 'identity' of the SENCO and the impact the NASENCO has on developing that in terms of *being prepared for the role*. Previous research has also focused on the 'status' of the SENCO (Cole, 2005; Layton, 2005; Szwed, 2007; Smith & Broomhead, 2019). In other words, *how they are perceived or regarded by others*. In contrast, identity (personal and professional) relates to *how the individual perceives and positions themselves within an organisation*. Focusing on status reduces agency due to factors beyond their control. Emphasising 'identity' brings influence into the realm of areas in their control as SENCOs. Limited consideration has been given to the prerequisite requirements to becoming a SENCO, what makes a SENCO effective (Dobson & Douglas, 2020a) in their role as a leader and what professional development is required beyond the NASENCO to sustain effectiveness (Smith & Broomhead, 2019) and retention.

> The SENCO Award does very little to prepare SENCOs for the role – we didn't study any particular special needs; didn't learn how to run annual reviews; didn't cover statutory assessment ... I could go on.
> – CD, Inclusion Manager on Twitter (13 April 2018)

Action task:

What would be your response to this SENCO on social media? Is the role about operational tasks or strategic leadership?

It should be noted, until my research, there was no defined leadership model to support SENCOs reflect on professional practice and areas for development.

> I don't think SENCOs are seen or respected as leaders enough.
> – SENCO (quoted from Devi, 2022)

The newly proposed qualification in September 2024 (NPQ SENCO) cites 'underpinning research' to support the presented guidance and framework from a positional perspective of 'Learn that' and 'Learn how to' (i.e. secondary research). In other words, the focus is a derived emphasis on knowledge and skills, not SENCO identity, agency or power for impact. Eight areas have been defined in terms of school culture, statutory framework, identification of needs, teaching, behaviour, leading and managing provision, professional development and implementation. The professional development element focuses on what SENCOs do for others, not their own professional growth.

 In your shoes:

Who would you choose from Table 4.2?

You might argue, it isn't always that simple. True. However, a person with the right attitude can acquire knowledge and skills. Someone with skills and knowledge cannot always develop the right attitude for leadership.

So, it boils down to how we perceive a SENCO and whether we place an emphasis on management or leadership (Mackenzie, 2007). Being a leader is not about positional recognition. It's about influence and building teams. Who are SENCOs primarily leading? We argue the case for SEND7 interactions (Devi & Bowers, 2022), however, *the primary*

*Table 4.2* Two candidates applying for the SENCO role

| SENCO A | SENCO B |
|---|---|
|  |  |
| Tania, who has a lot of SEND knowledge but struggles to carry herself as a leader. Not always able to develop teams or manage conflict. Well-meaning and passionate, eager to please, but seeks to change minds by doing it all and being at the centre. | Maria has limited SEND knowledge but can lead others by enabling them to develop their skills. Carries an attitude of being able to work with others and on her own. Can be innovative in problem-solving and always seeks to hear other people's views. |

*influence of SENCOs for school improvement leadership is teaching staff*. A well-trained teaching staff can then direct teaching assistants/support staff well and, through the demonstration of their actions and distributed leadership models, impact leadership more broadly.

Leadership is about change and SENCO leaders do not work in isolation. Therefore, the possibility arises of tension where other actors in the wider school setting (teachers and leaders) do not want change and therefore require the statutory role to be about managing the status quo (Douglas & Dobson, 2020a). This could create a work identity integrity violation or conflict (Pratt et al., 2006), leading to identity customisation (Curran et al., 2018; Curran et al., 2019; Curran et al., 2021). Struyvea et al. (2018) argue SENCOs as teacher leaders (in Scandinavia) engage in legitimate action when principals release power. In other words, senior leaders recognise the evolving nature of their own identity triad (Sherman & Teemant, 2021), allowing others space and opportunity to flourish too.

To consolidate the discourse in this area, let me share a possible trajectory I presented in my research as part of the findings (Table 4.3). The aspect of 'being part of the senior leadership team' will be addressed further in Chapter 7.

Trent (2011) argues extensively for an embedding period of three to five years for teachers to be truly immersed in their teacher identity, so as to impact other teachers. At the other end, Tissot (2013) purports a nine-year teaching experience period for SENCOs prior to being part of the senior leadership team (SLT). Some headteachers would both question and argue, what if newly qualified teachers came with leadership experience

TRANSITIONING FROM TEACHER TO SENCO

*Table 4.3* Four stages of the SENCO trajectory (Devi, 2022)

|  | Aspiration | Induction | Professional | Established – SLT |
|---|---|---|---|---|
|  | Three to five years of teaching experience | Completing the induction qualification, max three years | Implementing a vision, three years | Nine years plus in education |
| Rationale | Trent, 2011 | Legislation | Effective practice | Tissot, 2013 |

in another sector? That is a case-by-case judgement. However, at the end of the day, it is about leader-to-teacher credibility.

> *I have been a SENCO for almost 20 years. I learnt the most during the first 6 years and since then, it has been more about keeping up to date and moving on with good practice.*
> – SENCO Q47 (Devi, 2022)

 **Question:** How do senior leaders make the case-by-case judgement?

The SLIM Framework in Part 2 provides a possible solution.

## Summary

This chapter shared two models of teacher-to-SENCO transition and considered the longer-term trajectory over time from aspiration to induction to recognised professional and finally established member of the senior leadership team.

Chapter 5 examines two metaphors to support SENCOs in finding direction and staying on course in a turbulent and dynamic work environment.

PART 1

# 5 | How to anchor SENCO identity whilst doing the day-to-day job?

*SENCOs inevitably try to be all things to all people (SEND7), and in doing so, they often lose a sense of who they are and what is their role. This chapter takes a wider look at maintaining a sense of who they are when everything around the SENCO is changing. In this chapter, I propose two metaphors as ways of anchoring the direction of travel whilst not getting caught up in the day-to-day. Why two metaphors? The first metaphor is about facilitating the direction of travel and the second is about staying the course, having defined your direction.*

**It's a journey …**

Imagery is powerful. It helps us translate powerful (and sometimes abstract) concepts into tangible perceptions we can see and use within multi-perspective forums.

If we imagine the SENCO daily routine as a journey within a wider trajectory of institutional growth and personal development, we might think of Figure 5.1.

- The A to B straight line is the perceived institutional trajectory over time. It is the anticipated growth of a school or setting based on its improvement plan. We know, in reality; it is rarely that smooth.
- The heavy squiggle line is the daily routine journey of a SENCO. Many tasks loop back, remain unfinished or hit a dead end due to circumstances beyond the SENCO's control.
- The curvy hills and valley line represents the SENCO's own personal and professional development.

Looks really messy and stressful! I could have added recurring circles of caseload as a fourth layer pattern or other additional responsibilities SENCO often have (teaching designated safeguarding lead, deputy etc). This is when SENCOs come alongside families, parents or carers and walk with them in their journey.

This messy 'thought leadership' is the continuous experience for SENCOs on a daily basis, which is why many experience compassion fatigue or compassion stress (Paiva-Salisbury & Schwanz, 2022).

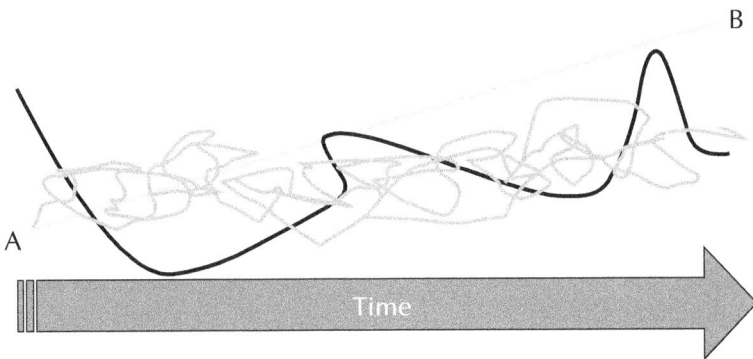

*Figure 5.1* Potential progress tracks in the life of a SENCO

> **Definition:** Adapted from Merriam-Webster dictionary (online: accessed May 2024): Compassion fatigue: the physical and mental exhaustion and emotional withdrawal experienced by those who care for [vulnerable] or traumatized people over an extended period of time.

The best analogy of the SENCO role is like walking in a dark tunnel continuously, without any real sight of a light at the end.

> *There isn't a career path within a school. The SENCO role is seen as an add on or lead into other roles Deputy Head/Head.*
> – SENCO Q69 (Devi, 2022)

> *I have been a SENDCO for 3 years now and in that time, I have learnt so much, much of this through experience and trial and error. There is no clear set out career path for me from here. At the moment, I am enjoying learning about this role and think that there is a lot more learning to be done. I would like to stay at this level for some time to feel that I am really good at the role but during this time I feel that my CPD will be largely down to me to decide on.*
> – SENCO Q30 (Devi, 2022)

**What's the answer?** Well, that depends on the question, but for now …

- *How do you support SENCOs to reduce compassion fatigue?*
    - Invest in SENCO wellbeing. Visit www.inclusionville.me.
    - Commission coaching and/or supervision. Engaging an external specialist helps to detach their freedom to be open, without linking it directly to performance and appraisal. (See Further Reading recommendation in Chapter 6.)

- *What needs to change?*
    - Read Chapter 7 and consider what your distributed leadership model looks like.
- *Is it possible for SENCOs to manage the increasing volume of workload?*
    - Possibly, but they are going to need support, so anchoring the SENCO identity in leadership is important.

The biggest game changer is empathetic leadership by the SENCO's line manager.

> Empathetic leadership … is 'not about taking IN CHARGE but about taking care of the PEOPLE THAT ARE IN OUR CHARGE'.
> – Miller (2022)

Case study:

Carlos is a Secondary SENCO. He also teaches part-time. He is given the equivalent of two days of SENCO time in the week; this is split into five segments across the week, i.e. a defined short period of time each day and sometimes two slots on one day sandwiched between his teaching. This is not ideal for Carlos, as he is constantly switching roles and hardly gets substantial time to get big pieces of work done. Most days, he leaves frustrated with the to-do list hardly scratched. This is not good for his wellbeing.

Top tips: For those who line manage SENCOs:

1) As complex as timetabling can be in schools, block significant periods of time for SENCOs so they can focus on the task at hand. In Carlos' case, two days as a block would be ideal or one day plus two half days.
2) Consider the transition between teaching and the SENCO role and vice versa. Is there a demarcation point?
3) Make time to listen, not fix or change. Just listen.

Top tips: For SENCOs:

1) Accept 'the inbox will never be empty' … this will help you leave at the end of the day and switch off.
2) Whatever time you are allocated for your SEND leadership, structure it so you are completing defined tasks at set times. These boundaries will help you manage the never-ending in-tray.
3) Read the biography of at least one leader (outside education) every year. This helps to ground you in knowing other leaders go through challenges too. The reason for something outside education – it broadens the mind and ability to transfer your own experience.

During the in-depth interview part of my research, I asked SENCOs to draw a freehand schema of leadership roles they undertake outside of school. There were many examples shared from the community, family or social group context. What was apparent, though, was a lack of transference of using these leadership skills and experience from an outside school context to the SENCO role. If, therefore, the role was defined in terms of skills, not just tasks and functions (SEND Regs, 2014, Regulation 50), would this engender broader transference from the induction qualification and wider experiences (see Part 2)?

Over the years, many have argued for a peer-to-peer mentoring model for SENCOs. For new SENCOs, this is something I am not in favour of.

Here's a scenario to explain why:

**SENCO A** (experienced): models good practice at her school. She mentions the headline process but omits to share the learning journey she has been on to get there and what 'contextual' conditions (see Figure 1.1) are in place for this to happen.

**SENCO B** (new): sees the outcome of the process SENCO A has described and sees it as a quick fix to the problem he is facing at his school. He fails to ask why SENCO A took that route, what alternatives were there and what challenges they faced along the way. So, at best, the transference becomes superlative as SENCO B is not only new to SENCO but also to the school. Hence, he is not aware of many historical, cultural and social factors (yet).

I think peer-to-peer mentoring for SENCOs works if:

a) The exchange is rooted in problem-solving dialogue, i.e. not just information gathering.
b) A line manager or someone responsible for governance joins both SENCOs in the conversation. This would aid in understanding broader applications.

Some of the most 'dangerous' SENCO peer mentoring happens online through social media. SENCOs post a partial problem and in return receive numerous and diverse responses, from which they have to sift through and consider the solution to the partial problem shared.

**Back to my two metaphors:**

**Setting direction:** A significant part of the steep learning curve for a SENCO is knowing the difference between strategy, long-term development plans and daily action plans. Having been in the classroom, many start with the micro, hoping this will help define the macro. It rarely does. However, SENCOs who start by knowing where they are and where they want to go usually can navigate a course from one to the other using their own North Star to guide them. Just like sailors at sea, SENCOs are experiencing continuous change from factors beyond their control and with little, if any, landmarks in sight.

What is the North Star in this context? Core principles and values defining decisions and choices of actions based on sound pedagogical knowledge and experience.

Action task:

It is helpful for SENCOs and their line managers to regularly discuss – what is their North Star?

**Staying on course:** The direction of travel has been set, but the unexpected happens! Something out of the blue that has the potential to change the course of direction lands on the SENCO's desk or in-tray. This is where having set an 'autopilot route' in place allows the trajectory to be steered back on course. Aeroplane pilots do it all the time!

Am I mixing my metaphors? Sea and sky? I would argue not. This is reflective of the way in which a SENCO leadership role is different from other leadership roles. It requires length, depth and breadth.

So, what is the SENCO autopilot route? Defined systems that embody the experience of what 'normal' looks like. Tasks and functions are subsets of systems. Most class teachers think in terms of tasks and functions because systems are either historical or led by SLT. This is part of the shift in thinking from being a teacher to a teacher-leader to SENCO (see Figure 4.2).

Case study:

Mandy, a primary SENCO, is constantly working evenings and weekends. Her to-do list never ends. She elicits the help of her line manager to help her create a better working environment and thereby be a more effective leader for the staff and children. Mandy's line manager suggests grouping the many tasks on her to-do list into 'activities'. This grouping activity subsequently leads to the refinement of systems that reduce workload and ultimately lead to better functioning. Instead of a linear to-do list that never ends, Mandy starts using circular activity lists. The result is no more late night working and her weekends are now freed up to be with her family. This intentional time-out feeds her wellbeing, and she has pause time, thereby breaking the enduring cycle of compassion fatigue.

Systems need to be developed and refined over time, but let me end this chapter with seven personal SENCO systems that could make a difference:

1) Define the working week and make time for rest. Rest is about doing something different that feeds your wellbeing.
2) Create periodic thinking time to reflect and learn.
3) Plan regular thinking time to look ahead and check your North Star.
4) Be intentional about professional development – less is more, as long as it is targeted.

# HOW TO ANCHOR SENCO IDENTITY DAY-TO-DAY

5) Connect with others and upskill them as you learn. This is a way of delegating through professional knowledge and skill exchange. It also frees you up to learn more and pass it on.
6) End each day/week with an intentional activity that signals 'switch-off' time. This could be a walk, a sit-down cup of something or just playing a song.
7) Be realistic when defining your strategic plan; only include three strategic aims. Getting the right three in place is far better than trying to half-accomplish five to six over a year.

 **Question:** Are there any more systems you would add?

 **Additional materials:**

- Reflective activity on direction and defining your North Star.

**Further reading:**

Brower, T. (2021). Empathy is the most important leadership skill according to research. *Forbes.* https://www.forbes.com/sites/tracybrower/2021/09/19/empathy-is-the-most-important-leadership-skill-according-to-research/ (accessed 14 May 2024)

## Summary

This chapter covered direction setting in a changing environment and how to stay on course.

Chapter 6 considers how to yield influence with the SEND7 and build trust.

PART 1

# 6 | What does it mean to leverage agency in order to improve standards of delivery?

*This chapter looks at yielding influence and using persuasion with the SEND 7 (i.e. in-house and externally).*

## Does persuasion matter?

The core of leadership is vision (direction) and values (North Star), as discussed in Chapter 5. Persuasion, as mentioned in Chapter 2, is about taking people on the journey with you. So, in this chapter, we are going to delve deeper into agency (i.e. influence).

Influence embraces elements of negotiation but not manipulation. Someone who negotiates demonstrates an ability to listen, weigh up different views, consolidate and problem-solve to pave a way forward that is beneficial for all. In contrast, manipulation is about 'this is my view' and I will do whatever it takes to make sure it happens my way! As already stated, identity (personal and professional) relates to how the individual perceives and positions themselves within the role and organisation, and agency provides the scope for this identity to be lived out in action through influencing others. The essential element connecting both is building teams. For power (i.e. degree of influence) to be real, there has to be congruency between identity and agency. If a leader is secure in their own identity, they can embrace different people's views, discern core aspects (through a values filter) and then find a solution. This is a learnt skill. However, it becomes trickier as the number of stakeholders increases. Negotiating can very easily turn into conflict management.

Meet two existing SENCOs from Inclusion Ville (Devi & Bowers, 2022).

LEVERAGING AGENCY TO IMPROVE STANDARDS

Penelope People Pleaser has a vision for how she would like to lead special needs and disability support across the school, but she is always worried about upsetting people. As a result, she often compromises her opinions and goes with either the most popular idea or, sometimes, the person who has spoken the most.

This does not evoke trust from the SEND7. In fact, many have now realised this is how she makes decisions, so they lobby other SEND7 members before a meeting.

Does Penny have any influence or is she just 'managing a difficult situation'?

Edward the Enabler invests time in knowing the people he works with. He knows what works for them and what presses their buttons. When a decision has to be made, he consults with everyone in advance, giving himself and them time to think. He goes into these meetings with an idea of what he thinks but is open to listening to new ideas. During a meeting, he states the purpose of the meeting (i.e. problem-solving), not just the agenda. Edward then summarises each person's view in relation to the problem, highlighting areas of consensus and points of difference. The conversation starts from a place of agreement, so there is scope to then address the areas where people have different perspectives. Everyone feels heard, even if their ideas aren't always the final decision.

## Who do you think leverages the most influence?

The nature of special educational needs and disability implies there will always be different voices and opinions. How this is handled is the hallmark of leadership. An individual can be in a position of status (i.e. on the senior leadership team) and still yield no influence. Identity, agency and power are internal dynamics that impact the outer world. Therefore, it is important to understand these dynamics within the SENCO world.

Professional agency emerges from identity (Clarke, 2009) and 'identity work' is an intentional series of actions that give rise to beliefs around professional, cultural, political and individual values. This provides an individual with a reference for themselves, as well as recognition by others. Formation and transformation of identity result in a

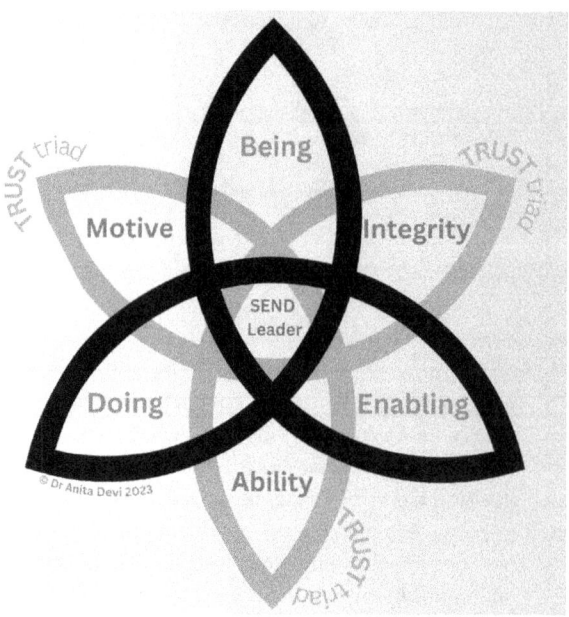

*Figure 6.1* Layering the trust triad on top of the three dimensions of SENCO action that need to work together for SENCOs to flourish (see Figure 4.3)

https://www.sencoleader.pro/

microscopic analysis of who one is, what they are doing and what they may become. Figure 6.1 builds an additional layer to the previous model of 'being, doing and enabling' (Figure 4.3). This second layer is a possible trust triad (see pages 17 and 88). Building trust requires the SENCO to authentically demonstrate their motive, integrity and ability. Therefore, identity consists of both stable and unstable identities (Day et al., 2006; Day, 2007; Sammons et al., 2007) within a wider evolving process of identity formation (Clarke, 2009) and adaptive practices to educational reform (see Figure 1.1). Agency can be both perceived and actual.

Within the primary school context of literacy, which text to use decisions, Jeffrey and Troman (2013) argue, are determined by three influences, namely experienced teachers' principles driving performativity, the creativity of new workforce members and wider societal influences. In praxis, this broadly translates to conversations such as, 'this is how we have always done it' (performativity of experienced teachers), 'here is a new idea' (creativity of the new labour force) and 'what's needed or required?' (industrial imperatives). Therefore, creativity can end up competing with performativity or industry-based accountability. Similar challenges apply to the SENCO world; within the confines of the law, there are the 'always one-way' people, the radicals with new ideas and those who ask, 'what is the bare minimum required?' In effect, discretionary effort can be compromised.

 **Questions:**

Pause for a moment and ask yourself, *how would you define the purpose of the SENCO role, and how does this come into tension with any wider educational agendas*? Make a list of these tensions and any other paradoxes you have observed.

 **Action task:**

It might be helpful to look up the difference between tension and paradox. Now re-read your responses to the questions above. Would you refine or change anything?

## My thoughts …

Let me share four tensions I've observed as a SENCO myself and in training other SENCOs.

#1 SENCOs seek to articulate and recapture aspects of the whole child and young person's personality that were once expressed in child development or childhood and that are not captured effectively by the prevalent educational standards discourse.

#2 The gap between initial expectations of the SENCO role and the actual lived-out experience of 'doing the job' can produce a reality shock (Kramer, 1975 cited in Yih, 2021). In other words, professional-aspirational values conflict with work-world values. This is an unrecognised loss, and 'where there is loss, there is grief' (Doka, 1989, p. 4). Doka further states there are societal norms and expectations about the expression of grief, particularly in a professional context.

#3 In the health world, there is a construct called 'private shadows' (Papadatou, 2000, p. 61), which embraces a wide range of unavoidable and painful experiences when health practitioners experience continual prolonged loss. How many SENCOs live in the 'private shadows' when a placement doesn't come through, resources aren't available or their voice is drowned out by others in the SEND7?

#4 The SENCO is required to be both visible and available. Yet the role itself embraces layers of invisibility. Many do not fully understand what the role entails from a personal perspective, as much emphasis is placed on 'tasks and functions'. Where is the individual in this? At another level, many SENCOs in my research shared they were invisible, inaudible, ignored, misunderstood and undervalued in their role. Imagine coming to work each day to this daily experience. That's why I stated in Chapter 2 that the SENCO role isn't for everyone. Legislation in England, however, requires every school (state sector) to appoint a SENCO. Have we lost sight of the purpose?

I have always challenged sector phrases such as 'the SENCO role is lonely' because I perceive leadership to be about building teams (my North Star), and if you have a team, you can't technically be lonely, or can you? Of course, it is possible to be lonely on a team. However, the word 'lonely' takes away from the 'leadership status' of building a team and having followers. For me, a better word than lonely is 'marginalised'. In other words, marginalisation describes the asymmetrical power relationship between two cultures (Park, 1928, p. 893 cited in Yih, 2021) with an associated lack of value placed on their work. They are more vulnerable to the experience of living between two or more levels in a hierarchy (Dickie-Clark, 1966, p. 366 cited in Yih, 2021). So, there is both an irony and a paradox here. *The very individuals pursuing inclusion across an educational setting are themselves marginalised.* One could argue this gives them better empathy for those they serve, but it can also be challenging. The wider system advocates 'person-centred' approaches (Sanderson & Lepkowsky, 2014), yet we do not see a person in the SENCO or vice versa, we see tasks and functions.

I raise these tensions, not to paint a gloom and doom picture but with the hope of driving change. The SENCO role is far more than a set of 'authority functions' (Regulation 50) and individuals who talk about this role and train, support or line manage SENCOs need to demonstrate empathetic leadership and listening (see Chapter 5). At regional and national levels, there also needs to be a broader recognition of how services like supervision should be made available for SENCOs if we are to retain them.

**New:**

In England, whilst the SENCO is a statutory role in public sector schools with mandatory training within the first three years, there is no central register to record who has been trained where and how many are still in the profession. Imagine if such a centralised register existed. How would this impact recognition, recruitment and retention?

## There is hope ...

As part of my research, I had to construct a conceptual framework that set a premise for positioning the SENCO in leadership. This framework positioned the qualitative methodology undertaken in the research but also highlighted significant gaps in the research literature to date. The conceptual framework embraced professional transitions, growth and the dynamics of a changing environment, as well as the interactions between these constructs. The aim was to use paradigmatic thinking (Kuhn, 1962) to analyse data in a new way of thinking.

The conceptual framework facilitated a process for applying the triad of identity, agency and power to the SENCO role, whilst recognising identity exists in multiples, is fluid and is socially situated (Sherman & Teemant, 2021). My conceptual framework sits on the social justice premise that all children should have access to high-quality provision, as stated in the United National Sustainable Development Goals (SDG4).

The spiral dynamic in Figure 6.2 provides a connective between the professional individual, the sector, the organisational workplace and future opportunities for career progression. Given that each of these four elements evolves over time, it gives rise to a spiral framework, where the SENCO leader can continue to develop in both inward and outward interest factors (identity) whilst contributing to the development of the organisation (agency) and wider sector (power). Figure 6.2 combines iterative systems and structures (beyond a SENCO's control) with evolution and adaptive approaches by the SENCO and their continuous identity work (Livingston, 2016).

Retention of the SENCO in post is critical (Pearson, 2008; Reid & Soan, 2019). From a social justice perspective, it ensures critical and scarce resources are not just allocated to the continual recruitment loop but are used to enhance support and provision for children and young people. Each new SENCO appointed (if unqualified) costs the school finances in ensuring they have met the basic statutory training requirement. The other vital reason for enhancing the retention of SENCO leaders is the intangible value of localised relationships that are built up over time in school with staff, and more importantly, in the community with parents and carers.

Over a 24-year period (1996–2020), a reoccurring dialogue has been the number of SENCOs seeking to leave the role, over what period (one to five years) and for what purpose (Male, 1996; Pearson, 2008 and Curran, 2021). The 2008 research was undertaken by the National Association of Special Educational Needs (nasen) using a postal questionnaire with 500 SENCOs in England. The length of service of respondents ranged

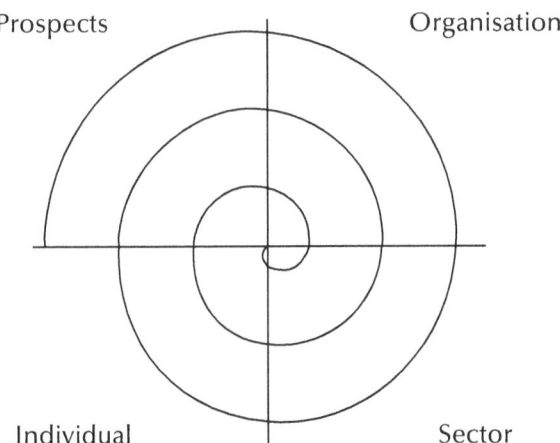

*Figure 6.2* Spiral model of growth for the SENCO leader that ensures ongoing individual development, sector-wide depth through enhanced inclusive practices in the organisation and long-term prospects for the SENCO in post (Devi, 2022)

from one year to 26 years; however, only seven had qualified teacher status at the time. Over half of the respondents (53.3%) did not want to continue with the role; 40% planned to retire within seven years and others due to heavy workload (Pearson, 2008). Fast forward ten years to 2018 and another nasen-led national SENCO Workload Survey in which 52% of 1900 respondents reported wanting to leave within five years, mainly due to workload (Curran et al., 2019). By 2020, the number had reduced to 27% in a much smaller sample (933 respondents) (Curran et al., 2021). However, the data does not reflect the same SENCO demographics between 2018 and 2020 so the comparison does not necessarily reflect an accurate decline. What the data does reflect over two decades (Pearson, 2008; Curran et al., 2018) is that retention is an issue and workload appears to be the primary factor. Hence, exploring two constructs becomes vital – leadership (Chapter 7) and continuous professional development (see Part 2).

Unfurling the four-dimension spiral in Figure 6.2 gives rise to a deconstructed cycle round, as demonstrated in Figure 6.3. The four dimensions embrace both leadership and opportunities for continuous professional development beyond the mandatory induction qualification.

The appointed SENCO brings individual capital to the role. This is where identity becomes relevant for the SENCO to have agency (within the sector) and power (organisationally) to influence their arena and sphere of influence, thereby enhancing their own prospects simultaneously for retention and advancement. However, without social

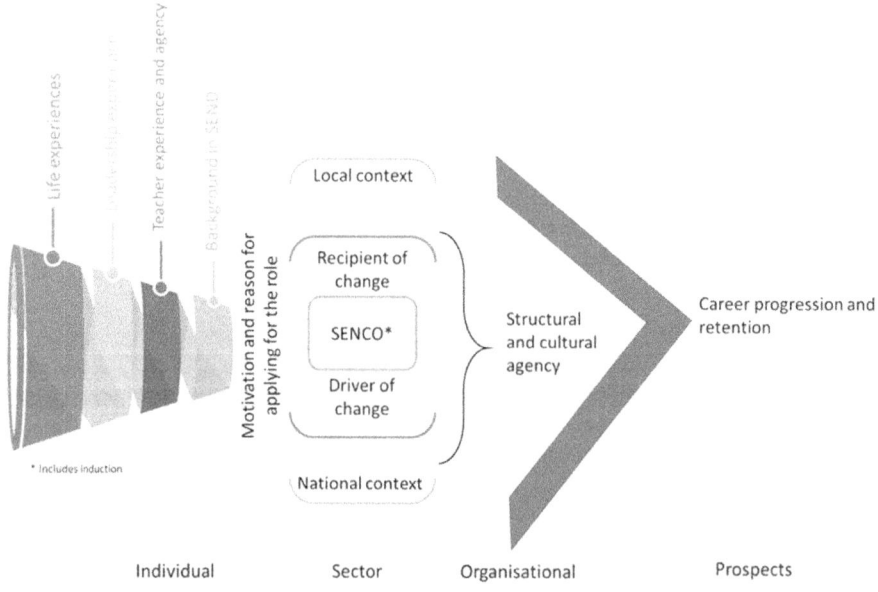

*Figure 6.3* One cycle of the spiral model that contributes to SENCO identity and growth (Devi, 2022)

capital, the SENCO remains ineffective. Using the three forms of social capital (Hallet & Hallet, 2010), Figure 6.3 recognises the potential of 'linking' capital in the 'sector'. Vertical dimensions are a core feature of linking sector capital by segmenting local and national context. If dense networks are overemphasised at the local level in policy frameworks, without connectivity to national oversight, or vice versa, this serves to deflate the SENCO as 'an agent of change' (Qureshi, 2014; Dobson & Douglas, 2020b).

Organisational aspects of the role that embrace structural and cultural agency for the SENCO to influence other leaders and teachers emancipate 'bridging' social capital for all young people (Hallet & Hallet, 2010). This outward-facing approach (Dobson & Douglas, 2020b) enhances leadership for learning (Hallet & Hallet, 2010). This is where continuous professional development (CPD) is critical, to strengthen not just individual linking and bridging capital, but also 'bonding capital', which strengthens the SENCO Community of Practice (Wenger et al., 2002). However, in a system reliant solely on 'unlinked' peer-to-peer capital support (Kosnik & Beck, 2011), the quality of such CPD could increase sector constraints and challenges. In other words, when building social capital is superseded by bonding social capital, an echo chamber is formed and hence many SENCOs talk of 'being isolated' (Mackenzie, 2013; Curran et al., 2018; Curran et al., 2019; Curran et al., 2021) when the very nature of their 'leadership' role is to lead diverse teams and operate from a place of inclusion. Examples of bonding social capital include the use of social media and always referring to the same sources instead of seeking different voices, creativity and innovation (Jeffrey & Troman, 2013)

None of this is simple or easy, nor should it be. Ultimately, we are discussing the leadership of some of our most vulnerable children and families in schools. In Part 2, I will deconstruct the practical application of the conceptual framework, as it emerged from the research data.

 Action task:

What are your top three takeaways from this chapter and how can you apply them to your context?

Additional materials:

- Reflective spiral.

 Further reading:

Rowe, J., & Sturt, P. (2023). *Using supervision in schools: A guide to building safe cultures and providing emotional support in a range of education settings* (2nd ed.). West Sussex: Pavilion.

**Summary**

This chapter considered the connectivity between individual linking and bridging and bonding capital to consider the SENCO as an individual, within an organisation, who exists in a sector where prospects for further growth need to be given due consideration.

Chapter 7, the final chapter in Part 1, considers legitimatised leadership and appointment to the senior leadership team.

PART 1

# 7 | How to define and manage power in order to drive change?

> It should be statutory that SENCOs are part of SLT because that is the only way they can influence change in their schools.
> – SENCO Q19 (Devi, 2022)

The quote above reflects a popular view held by many; however, those who advocate this have not really considered what it means in practice.

**Should the SENCO be on the senior leadership team or not?**

Look at Figure 3.1 in Chapter 3. Imagine if the successful candidate received an automatic and legitimised 'Go to SLT' pass, how would the headteacher and those responsible square this with other senior leaders who patiently climbed the leadership ladder? Would it be fair? How would the pay scale be calculated? This is a complex issue, and a blanket directive does not meet the requirements of every situation or every context.

For example, there are differences in senior leadership teams in primary and secondary settings. Similarly, the role of the SENCO (though a blanket term) differs considerably in early years, primary and secondary. I have been a SENCO in primary and secondary, and I have taught and worked with colleagues in early years. Each segment of pre-school and school-aged education involves different dynamics, different levels of expected independence and different levels of parental engagement.

There is also the question of maturity. This quote from my research intrigued me.

> When I sat down at the SLT [Senior Leadership Team] table, I was the only one other than the head who had actually done a leadership qualification. Which is a little bit worrying. When I pointed that out, they all suddenly wanted to do leadership courses, but it shouldn't be me, lower down in the pecking order, pointing that out.
> – SENCO I2

I asked the SENCO, 'How do you think the SLT responded to you saying this?' Their response: 'They were embarrassed'. The choice of language is also significant: 'lower down in the pecking order'. How much does it reflect a team or inclusive approach? This well-meaning SENCO had clearly much to learn about emotional intelligence (Goleman, 2005) in leadership. Tissot (2013) also noted that SENCOs most likely to be on the senior leadership team were those with at least nine years of teaching experience.

In England, the law, intended to liberate and elevate the 'status' of the SENCO role, subversively undermines it and inhibits the full professional development of the individual inward-facing interest factor (Dobson & Douglas, 2020a). The same study highlighted that interest factors were not influenced by organisational variables, such as the age group taught and school quality, as determined by government body-led inspections. However, Qureshi (2014) and other researchers (Szwed, 2007; Pearson, 2008; Hallet & Hallet, 2010; Oldham & Radford, 2011; Pearson et al., 2015; Done et al., 2016a; Curran, 2019; Plender, 2019; Curran & Boddison, 2021) continue to argue the need for affirmed 'leadership' status via membership in the senior leadership team. Reviewing the literature on SLT membership of the SENCO (2007–2019), Lin et al. (2021) conclude that SENCOs' views vary on this subject, and it is unclear whether this disparity relates to their roles and/or professional identities. Status is a positional value of a leader, or as Dobson and Douglas (2020a) have highlighted, driven by outward-facing factors. Status does not necessarily imply clarity of identity, agency or even power.

From the questionnaire phase of my research, the leadership teams' size across the sample surprisingly followed a bell-curve distribution with a normative average of four to five members. From the sample, 57 (51.82%) were part of the SLT, with 13 SENCOs (12.7%) joining for specific discussions, sometimes referred to as the extended SLT.

In Chapter 4, Table 4.3 proposes a timeline trajectory for the senior leadership team. For many, embedding knowledge and leadership provides stability.

A few further perspectives emerged from the research (Devi, 2022):

> *I became assistant SENCO in 2013. Inclusion Leader in 2016. Named SENCO 2018.*
> – SENCO Q76

There is a need to define the development of a SENCO beyond just SLT status. As without a trajectory of growth, SENCOS can 'feel' or remain stuck.

> *Slow; progression is non-existent. There is nowhere to go from here. At times, when it is too much and I want to drop the SENCO role (while keeping my teaching role), I am reminded that no one else wants it so there is no way out and there is nowhere to go from here.*
> – SENCO Q7

> *[You] can get stuck if [the] school [does] not see [a] need to have you on [the] SLT.*
> – SENCO Q27

My findings showed that whilst many were or had been on the SLT, they struggled to define 'who they were' or like SENCO Q29, they positioned their opportunities in hope:

'I have been promoted to a role on our SLT. I am hopeful that there is a wide array of opportunities'. The implication is that nothing has been evident yet. For others, the impact of being on SLT can still be hit-and-miss. It is 'very dependent on the views of SLT – [it] can plateau or be ... separated from [the] rest of [the] school' (SENCO Q97). In other words, simply placing a SENCO on SLT does not appear to add anything to their identity. It may give them status and a perceived wider sphere of influence, but as previously discussed, the additional responsibilities of being on the SLT often distract from SENCO priorities (Curran et al., 2021).

> *Personally, I have been fortunate as I have received ample training in both schools I have/am doing the role. The role has definitely become more strategic. In my previous school I was not on the senior leadership team – however I began to look for a new role in the summer term of 2019 and more roles are now advertised [on] the leadership team. This has its obvious benefits, but now as Assistant Headteacher a lot of my time is taken with the day to day running of the school and this gives me less time to concentrate on inclusion.*
> *– SENCO Q51*

## SENCO aspirations

During the interview phase of my research, SENCOs were asked to map their path over the next few years. Table 7.1 summarises seven key themes that emerged from SENCOs projecting themselves into the future.

Many saw the long-term goal as assistant head, deputy head or headteacher (SENCO Q17) or even local authority/national roles (SENCO Q37). Some argued, 'I only like moving on once I'm confident in what I'm doing now' (SENCO I24).

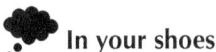 In your shoes:

**SENCO:** What are your mapped-out aspirations and who have you shared these with?
**Line managers:** Have you talked to your SENCOs about their growth trajectory (see Part 2)?

 Additional materials:

- SENCO aspiration planner.

Hallet (2021, p. 9) stipulates:

> Therefore even though the 2015 Code of Practice advocates that the SENCO should become a member of the Senior Leadership Team, the degree to which this makes a difference in practice depends upon the philosophy and courage of the SENCO alongside the cultural expectations of the educational settings.

*Table 7.1* Seven emerging themes around SENCO aspirations

| Aspiration theme | SENCO voice |
|---|---|
| On the SLT as a SENCO | <ul><li>*Probably still doing what I'm doing* [as] *a senior leader* – interviewee 2</li><li>*I would like to be more secure and have more ownership of my leadership within the school* – interviewee 7</li><li>*… just the same school I'm in but it being much more inclusive and open place because of my leadership* – interviewee 12</li><li>*SLT, here or elsewhere* – interviewee 15</li><li>*I could be a deputy head* – interviewee 19</li><li>*Leadership … [however] … this is a question that I've asked myself … do I want to stay in mainstream, or do I want to look at moving on and doing this in an advisory capacity working for an external agency?* – interviewee 26</li></ul> |
| On the senior leadership team doing a different job | <ul><li>*Deputy head (without any responsibilities for inclusion)* – interviewee 6</li></ul> |
| Leading with a wider level of influence | <ul><li>*Multi-Academy Trust SENCO* – interviewee 5</li><li>*A bigger team of people that can support delivery* – interviewee 11</li><li>*Sharing ideas and sharing good practice* – interviewee 20</li><li>*I would like to be working across both schools as a SENCO … [or] an educational psychology doctorate … I love my job at the moment, but I don't know if I can imagine myself doing it [long-term]* – interviewee 27</li></ul> |
| In a different school | <ul><li>*A SENCO in that school* – interviewee 3</li><li>*… if not in a specialist setting, I'd like to work with children who have special educational needs across a wider range in a mainstream setting. So, I am at the moment quite keen to move on* – interviewee 23</li></ul> |
| Full-time SENCO | <ul><li>*I would just like to be a full-time SENCO and I would like to be taking up that transformation project* – interviewee 8</li></ul> |
| Leave education | <ul><li>*I'm not going to be a SENCO anymore. In fact, I won't even work in education* – interviewee 16</li></ul> |
| Undecided | <ul><li>*I don't know whether I will still be a SENCO, or I will divert but still be involved in SEN* – interviewee 17</li></ul> |

Most SENCOs stated that no time, if any, had been invested in defining what SENCO meant in terms of identity and leadership within their setting. Reflecting on personal trajectories, participants felt the focus had been on 'getting the job done' (Woolhouse, 2015) rather than a deepening of personal and professional clarity. A variety of methods were discussed in terms of how this could be achieved through reflective journals, identity boards that use images to construct ideas and videos, to name a few. This was felt as something that needed to be part of the induction qualification and could contribute to the well-being of SENCOs. Skinner et al. (2021, p. 5) argue that 'teacher's professional identity and their competence and worth, achieved and mediated through interactions with others, are crucially involved in determining wellbeing'; the construct of SENCO wellbeing as a significant contributor and by-product of SENCO identity and agency (Devi & Bowers, 2022).

# HOW TO DEFINE AND MANAGE POWER

## Insiders or outsiders?

Another strong argument often put forward by advocates for legitimising SLT status for SENCOs revolves around the balance of power. In other words, not being on the SLT makes SENCOs 'outsiders to the flow of power' (Brueggemann, 1997, p. 2). However, the combination of the six dimensions of the SLIM Leadership Model (Devi, 2022) 'empowers' SENCOs to be coherent in their doings, sayings and relatings (Kemmis et al., 2013). They also take the SENCO out of the bubble (Hallett, 2021) and can create broader discourses around inclusion, as opposed to just focusing on SEND.

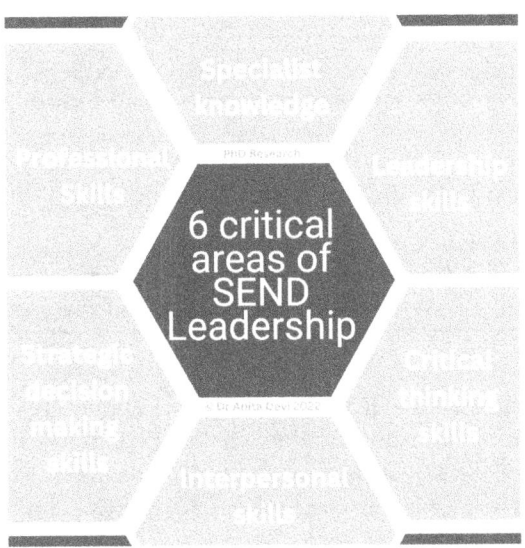

 **Question:** Do SENCOs need power or to be empowered?

## Line managing a SENCO

### Comments from SENCOs during the interviews (Devi, 2022)

> *Nobody else is qualified as a SENCO in the school so my line manager doesn't know really what my job is, and I have felt quite isolated.*
> *— SENCO I21*

> *We've just had a change in head teacher as well, ... and he's just swapped to be my line manager. So, I do think it will be easier now because I will be able to go directly to him, but they've not mentioned anything when I started about CPD really... I used to have a weekly meeting with a different line manager. But I would not call it a supervision or mentoring really, because I was teaching them. They didn't really understand, they wanted to find out more I think that's why they wanted to be my line manager, which was quite tricky.*
> *— SENCO I12*

Whilst little, if any, thought has been given to CPD for a SENCO beyond the induction qualifications, the same is true of those who line manage SENCOs. Line managers are there to support and challenge. They become accountability and encouragement

# 7 DIMENSIONS OF HIGHLY EFFECTIVE SENCOS

*Table 7.2* Four stages of the SENCO trajectory (Devi, 2022)

|  | *Aspiration* | *Induction* | *Professional* | *Established - SLT* |
|---|---|---|---|---|
|  | Three to five years of teaching experience | Completing the induction qualification, max three years | Implementing a vision, three years | Nine years plus in education |
| Rationale | Trent, 2011 | Legislation | Effective practice | Tissot, 2013 |
| Growth | <ul><li>Language and discourse</li><li>Activities and objects related to SEND Leadership</li><li>Patterns of relationships between people</li></ul> | | | |

partners. Yet many have very little understanding of how to do this or even the transition of their leader identity and agency into this significant role. With the current focus on SENCO 'tasks and functions' (Regulation 50), everything becomes about knowledge. In effect, it is possible for both the SENCO and their line manager to start 'in role' with a deficit 'self-concept'. Once again, this takes away from their agency to initiate change.

### Further training:

Accredited one-day course on effectively line managing a SENCO led by TeamADL (www.teamadl.uk).

Action task:

Make a list of the skills you think a SENCO needs to acquire and develop. Can you see any patterns by grouping them?

In drawing this chapter and Part 1 to a close, let us consider the SENCO Development Trajectory (Table 4.3 and Table 7.2) in relation to sayings, doings and relatings. Referring specifically to 'leading-for-inclusion: teacher talk' and 'male SENCO leadership', both Bristol (2015) and Pulsford (2020) respectively circle back to Kemmis and Grootenboer (2008) and Kemmis et al. (2013). Kemmis and her colleagues argue effective practice architecture is the intelligent and carefully constructed combination of 'sayings' (language and discourse), 'doings' (activities and objects related to SEND leadership) and 'relatings' (patterns of relationships between people). The question therefore presenting the sector is how do we continually support the development of SENCOs in terms of nurturing their identity, strengthening their agency and making power a construct for collaboration with the SEND7?

## Summary

This chapter starts by asking a difficult question, 'Should the SENCO be on the senior leadership team or not?' This closed question is not designed to divide the sector but to invite leaders to explore what this really means in terms of a SENCO career trajectory, as well as recruitment and retention. The definitive answer for each context and situation is circumstantial; however, SLT status shouldn't be assumed as an automatic rite of passage either. The chapter includes a broad range of perspectives from several SENCOs and suggests a skills-based model to help define a trajectory for professional growth. This chapter pulls together the preceding chapters in Part 1 and lays the foundation for practical application to be addressed in Part 2.

PART 2

# Introduction of the SEND Leadership Model

Welcome to Part 2. This is where we address the question – **So what?** In Part 1, aspects of research design, theoretical framework and the literature review informed the discourse. This section is more about what emerged from the data and how we can use it.

To date, there has never been a defined model about the individual who takes on the role of SENCO. In my research, I focused on the constructs of identity, agency, and power (Sherman & Teemant, 2021). As part of the interviews, SENCOs were invited to describe themselves through nine statements of identity beginning with 'I am …'

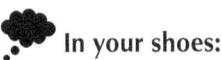 **In your shoes:**

Describe yourself with nine professional 'I am' statements – can you see any threads or patterns?

Interestingly, but not surprisingly, none of the SENCOs in the research stated, *I am a teacher, I am a SENCO* or even *I am a leader*. Instead, a greater emphasis was placed on defining SENCO identity through *doing*.

Some SENCOs expressed how the role had changed, and others stated how they were (emotional state) because of the doing and being taken advantage of by others.

> [I] swear a lot more … in my head … since taking on the role.
> – SENCO I8

> [I am] Taken advantage of. [I am] Tired of the paperwork. I want to work with the children more. I'm good at what I do when I have the time. It's always about that. Yeah, they're quite negative really.
> – SENCO I25

> I have been promoted to a role on our SLT. I am hopeful that there is a wide array of opportunities.
> – SENCO I29

It was clear from the responses across different elements of the research design that there was a need for more work on SENCO identity, as this is not SLT membership dependent, although the use of the word 'allowed' by interviewee 6 implies a hierarchy of expectation and permission.

> *I'm on SLT [now] but in my last school I was just a SENCO. Even then, I felt like a leader… you have to get point of view across, that inclusion point of view across. And I am allowed to, I'm not saying they always agree but. I have a vision of where I want our department to be.*
> – SENCO I6

Describing themselves through self-talk and self-perception (Neck & Manz, 1992; Quinteiro et al., 2016) during the interviews, many SENCOs found it difficult.

> *This is really hard. We're not often asked to talk about ourselves this way, are we?*
> – SENCO I15

> *This is a tough one, talking about myself.*
> – SENCO I5

A few recognised the need to perceive themselves as a leader, 'I would identify as' (SENCO I27). Whilst others expressed a compulsion to be something, 'I have to be' (SENCO I6).

A thematic analysis was undertaken of the 200+ statements received and what emerged were six identity themes (Figure P2.1).

The six themes reflect the intertwining of doings, sayings and relatings (Kemmis et al., 2013) for the SENCO role (see Table 7.2). It is also interesting to note that of the six themes, five are skills-based and yet when asked what additional CPD they would want, most SENCOs in this study focused on 'specialist knowledge', as this was perceived as a lever to enhance school-wide influence.

> *I would like to have more in depth training on various subjects as many stakeholders think that SENCOs are the font of all knowledge for SEN. They often don't realise that we are not experts, we have just done one extra course than a normal teacher …I would like to have more detailed training on things such as ASD, Dyslexia, other SEN needs.*
> – SENCO Q67

Each of these six themes was further deconstructed into four subthemes that helped to bridge the gap between transformational leadership (Bass, 1990; Hauserman & Stick, 2013; Jensen et al., 2018) and connected leadership (Hayward & Newman, 2014).

# INTRODUCTION OF THE SEND LEADERSHIP MODEL

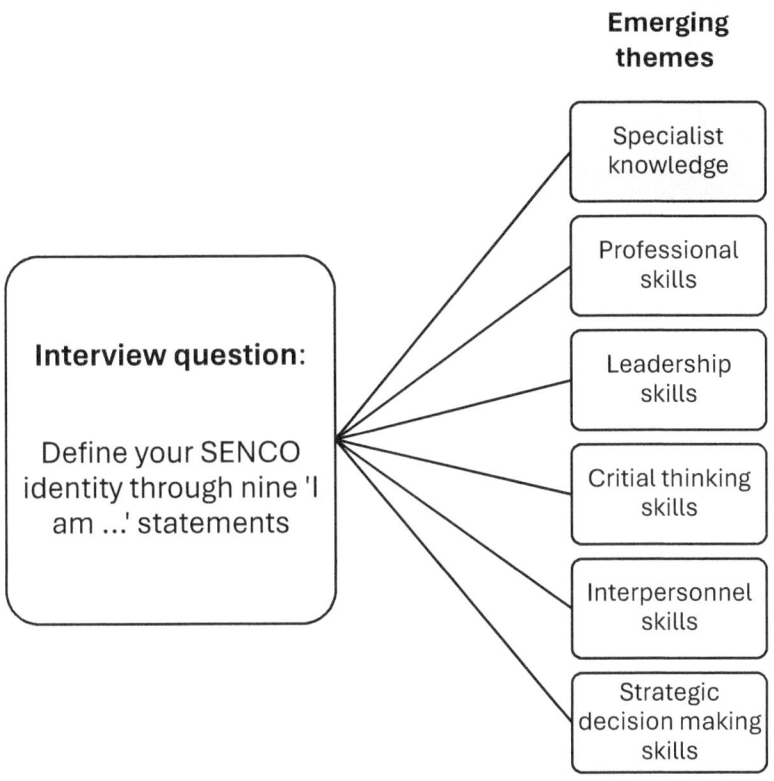

*Figure P2.1:* Six identity themes perceived as essential for SENCo identity and role (Devi, 2022)

Whilst Northouse (2019) makes the case that transformational leadership translates to the four factors of idealised influence, inspirational motivation, intellectual stimulation and individualised consideration, Tian et al. (2016) highlight that connected leadership embraces emotional capital, shared vision and purpose, and a focus on building relationships, not just maintaining them. In effect, the combination of these two models of leadership through the six themes and subsequent 24 subthemes brings together an identity, agency and power triad (Sherman & Teemant, 2021) for SENCOs.

SEND Leadership = Connected Leadership + Transformational Leadership

Therefore, the full SEND Leader Integrated Model (SLIM) can be viewed in Figure P2.2.

It should be noted that five out of the six dimensions all pertain to skills, which implies that growth and progress need not always be about doing more, but rather doing better.

# 7 DIMENSIONS OF HIGHLY EFFECTIVE SENCOS

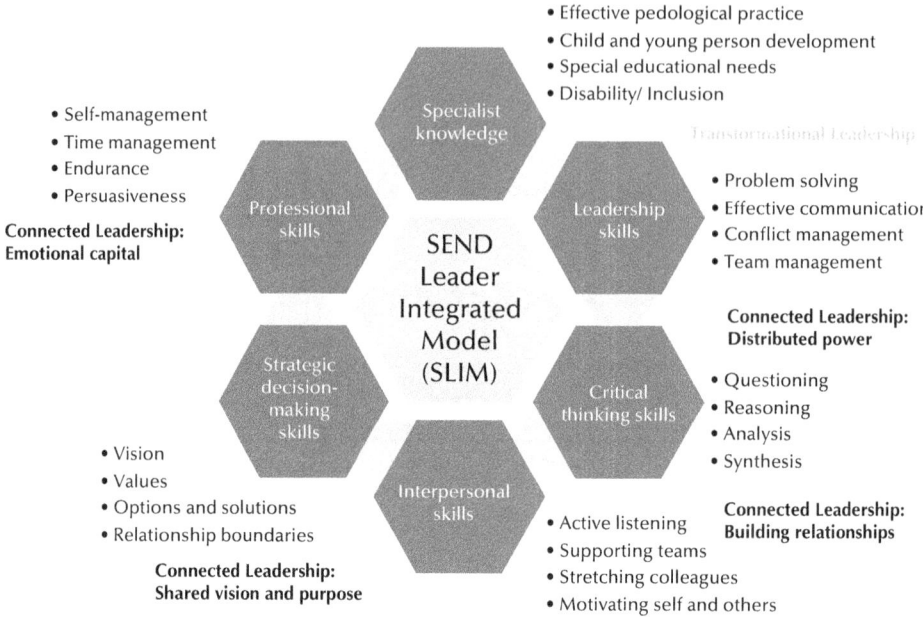

*Figure P2.2:* SEND Leader Integrated Model that embraces the six identity themes from SENCOs (Devi, 2022)

**Action task:** Before reading Chapter 8, jot some notes in Table P2.1 about your views on the six identity themes that go together to make SLIM.

*Table P2.1* Reflective questions around the six dimensions of the SLIM (Devi, 2022)

| Identity theme | What does this mean to me? | Why is it important? |
|---|---|---|
| • Specialist knowledge<br>• Leadership skills<br>• Critical thinking skills<br>• Interpersonal skills<br>• Strategic decision-making skills<br>• Professional skills | | |

## Summary

### *Transformational leadership (TL)*

Transformational leadership includes idealised influence, inspirational motivation, intellectual stimulation and individualised consideration (Bass, 1990; Hauserman & Stick, 2013; Jensen et al., 2018; Northouse, 2019).

SENCOs aren't just in office to 'maintain' a system. They need to be given leverage to transform it.

Specialist knowledge pertains to understanding broader frameworks around the child, their development and effective practices in the classroom. This also needs to align with legal frameworks around special educational needs, inclusion and disability. The question for practitioners, however, is which should be the starting point. The aspirations behind the 2014 SEND Reforms in England were child-centred, yet practice became about the law first. I would argue teachers and SENCOs need a solid foundation in effective pedagogical practice, child and person development and special educational needs linked to different aspects of children's development. The knowledge is then applied within the confines of the law. Creative ideas come when the 'should' leads the 'must' (SEND CoP, 2025).

## *Connected leadership (CL)*

Connected leadership (Hayward & Newman, 2014) embraces emotional capital, shared vision and purpose and a focus on building relationships not just maintaining them (Tian et al., 2016).

> *SENCos have a role to play in capacity building the system, not just reacting, but purposefully responding for growth.*

Whilst we know the most effective leaders work from the inner to the outer (Smart, 2013, 2023), the SLIM order clockwise round from specialist knowledge has been designed to support the transition and connection from teacher identity into SENCO leader identity and building agency along the way. In effect, placing strategic decision-making and professional skills as fifth and sixth relates to creating a sustainable model for growth. In other words, the order is significant for those 'new to SENCO', but beyond that the importance of the interconnectivity of all six dimensions should be seen.

In the next six chapters (Part 2), I will delve more deeply into each dimension, and in the final seventh chapter, I will consider how SLIM can be used to support a career trajectory for the SENCO. Each of the six dimension chapters contains an overview of the subdimensions, plus a Likert 1–5 scale of these can used for self-evaluation. The Likert scale moves through five moments of awareness, learning, knowing, applying and being confident. The scale is a moveable construct, as some years, depending on circumstances, a SENCO may feel confident; however, a changing situation the following year may reflect the need for further training or an upgrade in thinking. The main focus should be on continuous reflection for growth, not score accumulation. A SENCO achieving a 'perfect' score of 120 (i.e. 6 dimensions × 4 subdimensions × 5 max score per subdimension) is not necessarily desirable and could either reflect a bored practitioner or a gap in perception between aspiration and reality.

# 8 | Dimension 1: Specialist knowledge

PART 2

*This chapter positions specialist knowledge as a starting point, but not a sustainable point for SEND Leader growth. I therefore ask SENCOs to reflect on how much they need to know and how to keep up-to-date to be recognised as a leader of credible standing, but not someone who is solely responsible for special educational needs and disability in the setting.*

One of the most significant discoveries of my research was the revelation that many (if not the majority) of SENCOs intrinsically believe that if they show they have more SEND knowledge, it will improve their status as a 'leader' in their local setting. Yet, many also simultaneously admitted this wasn't true, as it just meant staff expected them to do more and teachers to do less. This is a paradox of the sector.

Hallet (2021, p. 2) supports this view, arguing that 'many SENCOs in England have always worked in theoretical and professional "bubbles" rendering them procedural experts rather than pedagogical leads'.

Status implies being highly regarded in another person's eyes. However, this is shifting sand. Identity is about the individual knowing who they are (strong foundation) and then demonstrating to others what can be done collaboratively.

### Do SENCOs need to improve their status or define their identity?

I would also argue the locus of control (Rotter, 1954) in 'identity work' (Clarke, 2009) is greater than 'status building'. Status building is endless with no real measure of success but constant people-pleasing. Identity work enables SENCOs to undertake reflective thought processes to create a personal schema of who they really are in the role.

Myth busting:

Knowledge ≠ leadership

# DIMENSION 1: SPECIALIST KNOWLEDGE

Leadership is primarily about creating teams and motivating people to act. To be treated like a leader, you have to act like one.

Finding a balance in this area is critical for the SENCO to be seen as having SEND expertise, but also then leading others to improve their practice, That's leadership. Currently, too many SENCOs see their role as 'stuck' in management, and the administrative side of management at that.

Specialist knowledge as a dimension is positioned in transformational leadership models in that its purpose is *to influence, inspire motivation (in self and others), provide intellectual stimulation for wider discussions with SEND7 and support individualised consideration during the assessment and identification process*. It is worth considering whether the current or proposed induction training embraces these four constructs of influence, inspirational motivation, intellectual stimulation and individualised consideration or just personal achievement.

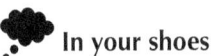 In your shoes:

**SENCO:** Reflect on the last training course your SENCO attended. What was the driver for attending?
**SLT:** What determines the level of specialist knowledge you think your SENCO needs?

> *You know I just do the things I like to do. And I'm not sure a career path is the right model. I think it's more about improving the status… It's that idea of you need to have the status elsewhere so that people go oh right oh yeah, we understand that.*
> – SENCO I13

One way of considering the specialist knowledge of a SENCO is to deconstruct it into four dimensions:

1) Effective pedagogical practice.
2) Child and young people development.
3) Special educational needs.
4) Disability and inclusion.

Action task:

**SENCO:** Consider your training over the last 12 months. Which of the four above did it cover? Is there an over-emphasis on one aspect?
**Line manager:** Look back over any training your SENCO has received recently, which of the four is mostly covered? Now discuss your observations with the reflections of your SENCO.

To manage and support the transition of teacher identity and agency into SENCO identity and agency (see Part 1, Chapter 4), we know sound pedagogical practice and an understanding of child and young person development are necessary for credibility and high impact in leading others.

To carry others with them on a journey of growth, effective leaders need to:

1) Adapt
2) Coach
3) Demonstrate
4) Empower
5) Enable
6) Instruct
7) Model

This is the purpose of acquiring specialist knowledge.

**Question:** Can you add any other observed behaviours you would see in a leader?

## 1. Effective pedagogical practice

**What is this?** This is about knowing what works in the classroom and how to adapt provision to meet a variety of needs. It brings together expertise in teaching with accurate knowledge of children and young people in the setting. This can also involve synthesising conflicting data (see Chapter 10).

**Why does it matter?** In terms of Regulation 50 (SEND Regs, 2014), effective pedagogical practice impacts identification, monitoring, advising, training, information gathering and securing additional services if needed.

To be effective in this area, SENCOs must not only draw on their own experience (making choices about practice and provision), but they must also be open to new ideas, reviewing new research around effective classroom practice and problem-solving, whilst enabling others to do the same (see Chapter 9).

> *I'm really thinking about how we can improve teaching colleagues understanding of children's learning in the classroom.*
> – SENCO I9

> *I am able to go into the classroom to show the teachers the best ways to work with these children. I think I'm understanding both the child's needs, and the teacher's needs within the classroom setting. I am proactive in identifying and getting the children the support that they need.*
> – SENCO I26.

# DIMENSION 1: SPECIALIST KNOWLEDGE

 **Further reading:**

Coe, R., Aloisi, C., Higgins, S., & Major, L. E. (2014). *What makes great teaching? Review of the underpinning research.* Project Report. London: Sutton Trust.

## 2. Child and young person development

**What is this?** There are five dimensions to human development, and these map onto the four broad areas of need stated in the SEND Code of Practice 2015.

The five areas cover physical, social, emotional mental health, sensory, cognitive and communication (Figure 8.1).

As part of their assessment approach, early years practitioners are highly skilled at using development milestones to track the progress of the child. However, as the child enters the compulsory education phase, this seems to stop and instead focus switches to curriculum acquisition and application milestones. From the child, to what they know – this is the threshold of stepping into formal education. However, curriculum attainment and achievement should ideally be considered alongside child development.

Each of the five dimensions of human development has its own trajectory and defined expected growth points. However, development isn't always uniform, and occasionally there is a delay in the development of one area. This does not necessarily imply the child has a special educational need or a disability. It may be a case of further practice,

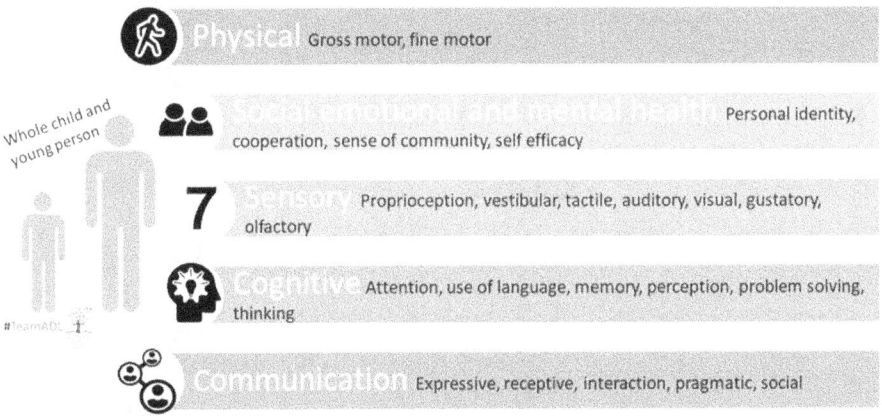

*Figure 8.1* Five aspects of human development, with subelements that affect learning defined for each

application of scaffolding theory and zones of proximal development (ZPD) or intentional learning opportunities are required. When progress is hindered, support for the child's continued learning depends on a team effort of the class teacher, the SENCO and parents/carers, who adopt the collective and collaborative role of the 'more knowledgeable other' (MKO).

In some cases (known as complex needs), the chronology of development is mixed up.

To ensure holistic assessment and identification take place for a child with SEND, it is important to consider the overlap of the four broad areas of need (Figure 8.2). Sadly, national data collection systems focus on primary need and secondary need. However, in this, the fullness of the child can be lost, and what is required in terms of co-ordinated support is lost. Most EHCPs cover the broad four areas of need; however, not always in an integrated manner.

**Why does it matter?** Knowledge in this area is vital for accurate identification and early intervention. SENCOs need to be able to advise teachers and parents as to whether a child is meeting child-related expectations (Regulation 50) and then discern developmental approaches and chronology in terms of curriculum delivery. Recent assessment guidance from government departments is beginning to recognise how children and young people with SEND can make horizontal curriculum progress, even if not reflected in vertical progress outcomes.

I would argue that this is a core area where SENCOs need to demonstrate in-depth expertise to synthesise data to make informed decisions.

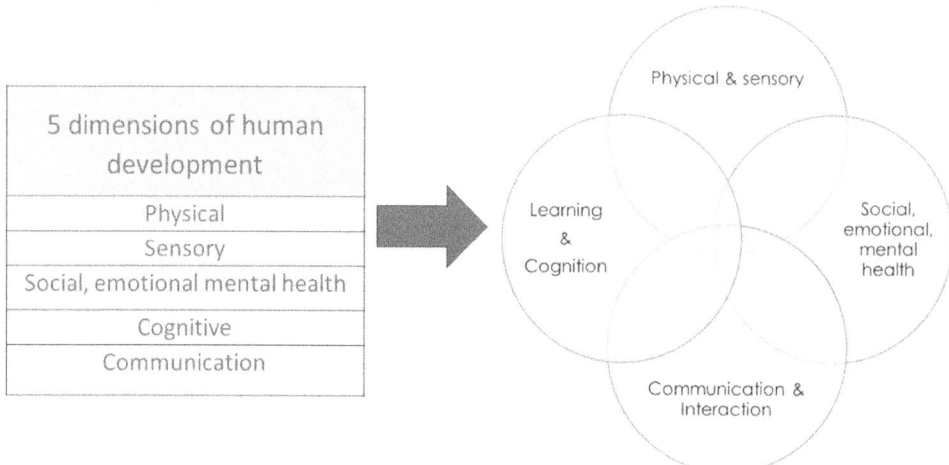

*Figure 8.2* Five aspects of human development mapped onto the four broad areas of need (DfE, 2015)

# DIMENSION 1: SPECIALIST KNOWLEDGE

*advising teachers about differentiating teaching methods. Sometimes it's to do with teaching methods and sometimes it's to do with behaviour management.*

– SENCO I23

*I know where the children need to be.*

– SENCO I25

**Further reading:**

Devi, A. (2020). (Series Editor Hollis, E.) *Essential guides for early career teachers: Special educational needs and disability*. London: Critical Publishing.
Devi, A., & Jagger, S. (2025). *Neuroplasticity and neurodiversity in the classroom.* London: Critical Publishing.

**Further training:**

SEND in the Classroom (2022) *Accredited Course on the Four Areas of Need by High Speed Training.*

## 3. Special educational needs (SEN)

**What is this?** This embraces aspects of legislation, policy (national and local) and practice (in-house and authority-wide). Two key elements of the process involve the graduated approach and four areas of need (Department for Education/Department of Health, 2015): both dynamic processes and entities (refer to Chapter 6 in Part 1).

Once again, the knowledge by itself isn't enough. It is the bespoke application that matters. Two children formally diagnosed with the same special educational need can present very differently. So, adding to Figure 1.1 in Chapter 1, an additional dynamic is 'the child' – their development and needs (Figure 8.3).

**Why does it matter?** It is in this aspect of specialist knowledge that a SENCO's ability to be agile with data comes to the forefront. Misidentification is costly and not responding in time can have a negative impact on the child or young person and their learning.

*I think I am successful. I hear rumours that oh, so and so mentioned you or your school at this particular thing. And I think we do in terms of our SEN and EHCP children; we get most of our children from out of catchment because they are making, their parents are making the proactive choice to send their children to us.*

– SENCO I20

# 7 DIMENSIONS OF HIGHLY EFFECTIVE SENCOS

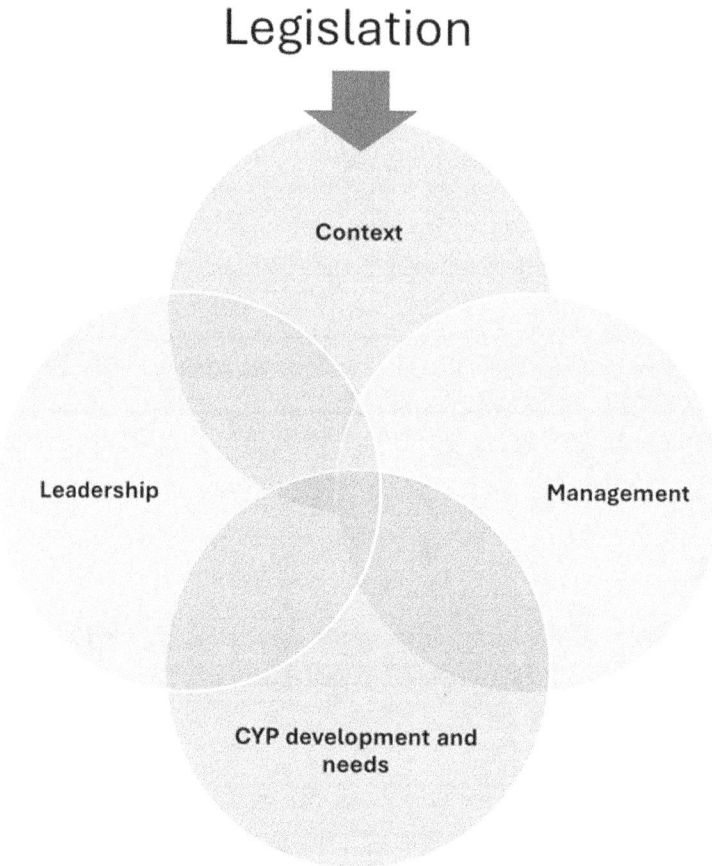

*Figure 8.3* Understanding the interaction between national legislation, local setting/context and the SENCO role (both leadership and management) plus child development and needs; whilst legislation is static, four areas remain dynamic.

 **Question:**

Focusing on the paperwork, have we lost sight of what really matters and how agile and responsive we need to be as educators? Additional provision isn't about 'more resources'. Sometimes it is about doing things differently in a timely manner.

## 4. Disability and inclusion

**What is this?** Whilst SEN is about responsive provision in relation to a need (often, but not always temporary), disability (D) is about proactive forethought to a condition that affects long-term active participation in everyday life. This forethought in action is called a 'reasonable adjustment' (RA). In other words, with the lens of ensuring everyone is included, a small adjustment to the environment and ways of working can make inclusion possible. In the United Kingdom, disability legislation is positioned in the Equality Act 2010, which prevents discrimination in relation to nine defined and protected characteristics. These include:

1) Age
2) Disability
3) Gender reassignment
4) Marriage and civil partnership
5) Pregnancy and maternity
6) Race
7) Religion or belief
8) Sex
9) Sexual orientation

Prior to 2014, in England, SEN and disability were defined by two different pieces of legislation. The Children and Families Act 2014 brought these two together without a coherent theoretical framework (Castro & Palikara, 2016). Thus, causing much confusion in the system and a lack of 'legal' clarity in the courtrooms between SEN and disability.

Inclusion is much broader than just SEND and encompasses a wider vision of community engagement and the long-term aspirations of the young person.

*I am a champion for inclusive learning within my school.*
– SENCO I13

**Why does it matter?** Many SENCOs would consider themselves to be advocates for the underserved or those with the most needs. Within the SEND7, this can cause many tensions. For example, if they are advocating for the child/young person and their families but are employed by the school or multi-academy trust, which comes under the enactment of national legislation through local government agents, this is where the 13 questions that Essex et al. (2019) asked trainee teachers become relevant. In particular to my research, the five most significant were:

1) What teaching strategies for inclusion have you learnt about during the PGCE (teacher training)?
2) In what ways has the university-based work prepared you for inclusive teaching?
3) Were there any aspects of inclusion taught in university that appeared to be at odds with what you saw in school?
4) Are there any groups at risk of underachievement that you don't feel confident to teach effectively yet?

5)  What do you understand by 'inclusion in teaching'? Which specific groups of learners (if any) do you think stand to benefit from an inclusive approach to teaching and learning?

If these remain unresolved for a teacher into their third year of practice, becoming a SENCO only serves to enlarge these conflicts in the psyche of the individual. The potential conflict (individual vs institution values) in practicum is particularly drawn out in the third question (DeLuca 2012; Gavish 2017).

## Self-audit grid for discussions with line managers

Table 8.1 presents each of the four dimensions of specialist knowledge, building in the capacity for growth if circumstances change, year on year. In Chapter 14, I provide a case study example of how this could be used with the other six dimensions of SLIM (Devi, 2022).

Read through the descriptors along the rows and *choose the best fit for this moment in time*. There is no right or wrong answer. It is about knowing where the SENCO currently is and what the potential for growth is.

Once the SENCO has completed this, I would suggest talking through the self-audit with their line manager. In particular, asking if they agree and jointly considering what evidence would support the best-fit judgement.

The discussion should raise further discussion points, such as what are the opportunities for growth? What further support is required? Does the SENCO exhibit a high level of leadership behaviours in an outside setting and is there potential for transference to school? For example, the SENCO might say:

> **SENCO in relation to effective pedagogical practice (score 5):** *I am confident coaching others in my voluntary capacity, but I find it hard in school as a SENCO.*
> **Line manager**: *Why is that?*
> **SENCO**: *I really do not get much time to do this.*
> **Line manager**: *Tell me more.*
> **SENCO:** *Most of my time goes into chasing teachers to support students through the strategies listed on the SEND register. No one listens.*
> **Line manager**: *Do you think, if you adopted a more coaching style with the teaching staff, they might embrace the strategies you know the students need?*
> **SENCO**: *Possibly.*
> **Line manager**: *What do you do to support coaching outside of school in your voluntary role that you could use in your SENCO role? How can we support you to do this?*

Table 8.1 Five level descriptors for segments of the specialist knowledge dimensions (Devi, 2022)

|  | 1<br>Aware | 2<br>Learning | 3<br>Know | 4<br>Apply | 5<br>Confident |
|---|---|---|---|---|---|
| Effective pedagogical practice | I am aware of what strategies work in the classroom, and I try to keep myself up to date with the latest research. | I am learning to explore broader ideas around effective classroom practice that supports additionality and reasonable adjustments. | I know how to communicate a range of different pedagogical approaches to colleagues, highlighting the most effective for the needs of the child and a group of children. | I can apply my own understanding of classroom practice to support teachers and teaching assistants in managing increasing needs in the classroom. | I am confident in modelling, team teaching, mentoring, coaching and training teacher colleagues and teaching assistants about inclusive practice in the classroom. In doing so, I am confident we can together build capacity to be inclusive for all. |
| Child and young person development | I recognise child and young person development plays a role in accurate identification for SEND, but I am not sure how. | I am learning more about the development milestones and how this applies to learners in my setting. | I know the four broad areas of need (SENDCoP 2015) linked to child and young person development. I can see and articulate the synergy of this interaction to others. | I can apply different development milestones to create an accurate picture of the child or young person's needs, including the next steps. | I am confident in discussing developmental milestones with staff and parents so that together we can develop a better understanding of the child or young person's needs and further progression. |

(Continued)

Table 8.1 (Continued)

| | 1 Aware | 2 Learning | 3 Know | 4 Apply | 5 Confident |
|---|---|---|---|---|---|
| Special educational needs | I understand the basic concepts of legislation/national policy; the four broad areas of need and the graduated approach cycle. I know how to research different needs that present themselves in our setting. | I am learning to deepen my own knowledge of SEN, giving due consideration to how I communicate and share this with others in a meaningful way. | I know how to support increasing numbers and the range of needs in the classroom. I am able to share this with teacher colleagues in a way that doesn't increase workload, so it is manageable for all. | I can apply my insights and knowledge to continually reflect and refine how we support learners in the classroom and in other learning activities. This includes how we communicate with family/home. | I am confident in sharing my knowledge about a range of needs with mixed audiences, taking into account their background and level of expertise. |
| Disability and inclusion | I recognise the importance of inclusion and being proactive in our support for those with disabilities (overt or hidden). | I am learning to have a deeper appreciation of how to adapt practice to increase our approach to being inclusive, as well as how to communicate change to colleagues. | I know the legal responsibilities we uphold, where we are at and what further work needs to be done going forward. I also know how to lead and work with others in achieving our goals for inclusion and disability awareness. | I can apply my experience and knowledge of disability and inclusion to respond sensitively to any new needs that arise. | I am confident in talking to those responsible for governance about our approach towards inclusion and disability, including what's working, what's not and what needs to change. I am comfortable with being questioned about this and responding confidently. |

SLIM (Devi, 2022): Specialist knowledge: Transformational leadership

The self-audit has led to a learning conversation for growth.

Out of the six dimensions of the SLIM, specialist knowledge is the only one that is knowledge-based. The rest are all about skills. However, knowledge on its own has no value. In the case of leadership, knowledge needs to be shared effectively to empower and enable others. This is when a knowledge-based leader becomes a transformational leader.

As a leader focused on transformation, the SENCO is using knowledge to drive change at three levels: first, for the child and young person; second, in practice, i.e. what teachers do in the classroom; and third, increasing the capacity for inclusion across the setting.

Given the complexity and the gravity of the specialist knowledge required, a teacher with only one year of teaching experience would not be suitably placed to take on the role of the SENCO. Hence, there is a need to ensure the retention of SENCOs within a framework of career progression, as outlined previously.

## The role of an induction programme or qualification

The NASENCO, NPQ SENCO or any other qualification/induction programme for a SENCO programme should begin to address the dimension of specialist knowledge. However, it is worth noting two points here:

1) Specialist knowledge without leadership skills is ineffective.
2) Any induction programme/qualification is just an initial taster. It provides only a segment of the wider learning to be undertaken. It would be bizarre to state that all a strong marriage really needs is a wedding service (appointment) and a honeymoon (induction programme). Marriages require growing investment and growth by all parties and the collective every day. The wedding and honeymoon form the foundation for much more to come.

### ❌ Myth busting:

All I need to be a highly effective SENCO is to complete the induction qualification.

This is inaccurate because it assumes that front-loading a SENCO with knowledge will sustain, retain and develop them in their career journey. This is not true for any vocation. Therefore, the case for a SENCO leadership framework for ongoing development is imperative.

*Table 8.2* SLIM (Devi, 2022) specialist knowledge recording table over five points in time

| Date |
|---|
| Effective pedagogical practice |
| Child and young person development |
| Special educational needs |
| Disability and inclusion |

 **Action task:**

Use Table 8.2 to record your scores at four different points in time. This could be done annually as part of appraisal conversations.

 **Question:**

What are your top three takeaways from this chapter?

## Summary

This chapter evaluated the positional value of specialist knowledge in relation to leadership skills. Existing myths were challenged and the learning power of growth conversations between a SENCO and their line manager was presented.

Chapter 9 delves further into leadership skills by examining related behaviours and communications with others.

PART 2

# 9 | Dimension 2: Leadership skills

*Leadership is an intentional behavioural activity. Leadership is an acquired skill that builds on the 'self-knowledge' and ability of the individual. Therefore, being committed to learning leadership skills and learning from other leaders is critical.*

Let's begin by clarifying definitions:

- A **leader** is someone who directs, guides or conducts with authority and influence (identity).
- **Leadership** is about the actions and capacity to lead (agency).

**A timeless question:** Are people born leaders or is it something that is nurtured in them?

**My response:** Yes!

I haven't answered the question with a definitive response, as the question highlights a paradox. It's both! If we believe in the aspiration of inclusion, then part of that acceptance is believing each of us is distinctively made with a purpose and has a specific story to tell. I personally believe human creation is a matter of 'awe and wonder'. According to WorldoMeter (May 2024), the current world population is 8.1 billion people. That's 8.1 billion unique individuals walking on this planet, each with their own story, purpose and destiny. A baby arrives with more bones than they will have as an adult. Babies are born with approximately 300 bones that fuse together, as adults we have just over 200. We cannot describe this phenomenon in terms of 'how is this possible'. Yet we can observe 'how it is'. As well as physical differences, 8.1 billion people have distinctive personalities, born under distinguishing circumstances that mark our life stories and we each have matchless fingerprints! Not all are born to lead, but history highlights many who were not destined to lead end up being world changers.

Action task:

Make a list of the leader biographies you have read. What did you learn from each one and what have you applied to your own context? (Look at the top tips in Chapter 5.)

 **Top tips:**

1) Subscribe to a few non-education leadership podcasts. What can you learn and transfer to your role?
2) Save on your browser bar three favourite Leadership TED Talks that you can watch over and over to go deep into learning and apply this to your context.

A core element of leadership is discovery, which emanates from professional curiosity: asking questions and making sense of the answers we receive in relation to what we have known previously. Sometimes, the answers confirm our hypothesis of the world, and at other times, our worldview is changed through a paradigm shift (Kuhn, 1962). Isn't this the basis of learning in the classroom too? 'Leadership skills', as a dimension of SLIM (Devi, 2022) is the pinnacle for fusing both transformational leadership and connected leadership.

**Reminder:** From Part 2 introduction:

- **Transformational leadership** translates to the four factors of idealised influence, inspirational motivation, intellectual stimulation and individualised consideration (Northouse, 2019).
- **Connected leadership** embraces emotional capital, shared vision and purpose, and a focus on building relationships, not just maintaining them (Tian et al., 2016).

From a place of rooted identity, a SEND leader can lead other teachers to be secure in their identity as teachers, who demonstratively advocate inclusion in their classrooms. This is shared agency. Equally, as part of connected leadership, SENCOs can own their leverage of power and distribute it.

 **In your shoes:** As a SENCO, answer these three questions about yourself (at work and wider) and discuss your answers with your line manager.

1. What is important to me? List five things.

2. What do others think of me? Ask others.

3. How best to support me? List three things.

Some of you may recognise these questions as the pillars of a one-page profile person-centred tool that we use with children and young people. I have found it also very useful with trainee teachers and leaders. Understanding the rationale and use behind these helps.

# DIMENSION 2: LEADERSHIP SKILLS

| Question | Purpose |
|---|---|
| What is important to me? | Each of us places a different priority on what we value. Shared priorities become the basis for friendship and relationship building. Imagine if I shared with you that my five things included family and travel. This would give you a basis for knowing me a little deeper. Equally, if I said, 'Drinking a glass of wine each night', you would have a basis for concern and possibly challenge me by stating, 'Anita, wine may be important *to* you, but what is important *for* you is your health!' You have honoured my choices but also warned me about not being excessive in my consumption.<br>*(Let me put to rest any rumours: I do not drink a glass of wine each night. This was just a made-up illustrative example.)* |
| What do others think of me? | When we ask other people what they think of us, we discover they often place us in a much more favourable position than we see ourselves. The surprise of this adds to our joy. We are looking in-out and often through the meta-narrative in our minds. But others see us from out-in. We are going wider and they are going deeper. In times of difficulty and challenge, it is depth we need to restore balance. |
| How best to support me? | Most people if you ask them what they need, know. The problem isn't knowing; it is often expressing it and accepting the support. We all need support and help of some kind. Whether you are leading a nation, the wealthiest person in the world, a homeless person or someone with an addiction – we all need support and other people around us. Therefore, it is far better to ask upfront and say what is needed. Over the years, 'imposter syndrome' is a concept that has come into the leadership arena. We recognise that it is a psychological occurrence born out of doubt about skills, abilities and accomplishments. But if we dig deeper, it is also about adopting the lens of 'perfectionism and independence'. Yet, in reality, being perfect and self-sufficient is a mirage. A great antidote to 'imposter syndrome' is trusting a few selected people and asking them for support. |

## SEND: whose job is it?

I'm reminded of a famous story that has many versions, but basically, the gist is:

> *This is a little story about four people named Everybody, Somebody, Anybody and Nobody.*
>
> *There was an important job to be done and Everybody was sure that Somebody would do it.*
>
> *Anybody could have done it, but Nobody did it.*
>
> *Somebody got angry about that because it was Everybody's job.*
>
> *Everybody thought that Anybody could do it, but Nobody realised that Everybody wouldn't do it.*
>
> *It ended up that Everybody blamed Somebody when Nobody did what Anybody could have done.*

*Everybody is responsible for SEND.*

*Anyone can contribute.*

*Nobody needs to feel left out.*

*BUT Somebody (the SENCO) needs to lead.*

Now re-read the story, replacing Somebody with a SENCO:

> This is a little story about four people named Everybody, *a SENCO*, Anybody and Nobody.
> There was an important job to be done and Everybody was sure that *a SENCO* would do it.
> Anybody could have done it, but Nobody did it.
> *The SENCO* got angry about that because it was Everybody's job.
> Everybody thought that Anybody could do it, but Nobody realised that Everybody wouldnt do it.
> It ended up that Everybody blamed *the SENCO* when Nobody did what Anybody could have done.

Sound familiar? For many years, the educational sector rhetoric has been focused on two mantras:

> Every teacher is a teacher of SEND and every leader is a leader of SEND.

I personally do not like the language in either of these statements. Firstly, both these statements assume a sentiment of automaticity. I would argue that all teachers and leaders 'have a responsibility' to support and include SEND; however, the skill, knowledge, experience and expertise with which they can do this will differ. In an ideal world, long-standing teachers should be more adept; however, we know this is not always the case. I have worked with headteachers who have progressed through their careers never truly having understood the foundations of SEND. My second reason for not accepting the premise of both these statements is that it undermines the role of a SENCO. If everyone is either a teacher or leader of SEND, what purpose does the role of SENCO serve? We end up with a scenario of nobody doing what anybody could have done.

Therefore, as previously stated in Part 1, all teachers and leaders have a 'responsibility' for supporting and developing SEND provision to meet the needs of children. Responsibility implies an active process of engagement by all, with a SENCO 'somebody' leading it. Distributed leadership is a flatter leadership model that starts from the leader knowing

## DIMENSION 2: LEADERSHIP SKILLS

they have both power and agency to affect change, and through a range of strategies, they share this agency and power to ensure everyone is involved.

The leadership skills and attributes that emerged from the SENCOs in my research focused on problem-solving (Mintrop & Zumpe, 2019), effective communication (Momeny, & Gourgues, 2019), team management (Solberg et al., 2021) and conflict management (Wanjiru, 2021; Deshini et al., 2021).

These four pillars form the basis of the leadership skills dimension in SLIM (Devi, 2022):

1. Problem-solving
2. Effective communication
3. Conflict management
4. Team management

## 1. Problem-solving

**What is this?** As stated in Chapter 3, teachers are continuously making day-to-day decisions. This is true of most of the 8.1 billion people on Earth.

- What shall I wear today?
- What to eat?
- What should I say?
- At what time should I go to sleep?

There are micro-decisions, like the examples above, that are often automated, made for us or determined by other factors. There are also macro-decisions. These are the intentional choices we make that have significant consequences for ourselves and others. Decision-making is a learnt and practised skill through trial and error and perceived forethought of potential risks or consequences.

Decision-making is the by-product of a recognised problem. In effect, problem-solving affects every aspect of life. Sometimes those crossroads moments are more dramatic, and at other times, we recognise the road we are on and know what to expect.

 **In your shoes:**

SENCOs, reflect on your last SENCO working time. Make a list of all the problems you solved and the decisions you made. Are you surprised and what impact does this have on your cognitive and emotional wellbeing? What could you do differently?

### Why does it matter?

Problem-solving in leaders needs to be even more finely tuned. Why? There is much more at stake. Lives and resources are impacted, and the risks are high.

Problems can be solved in a variety of ways, but fundamentally they require head–heart connectivity. Being anxious, lacking calmness or even excessive slack can impede problem-solving effectiveness.

Solving a problem starts with gathering information from various sources. Ordering this information is vital for deciding – What next?

As SENCOs become more experienced, we would expect to see an increase in tacit knowledge. These are decisions rooted in context, experience, practice and values. Tacit knowledge is difficult to communicate, as it resides in the mind of the leader. Yet communicating it is imperative to increase the shared capital of tacit knowledge and to ensure SEND doesn't become the responsibility of just one person.

Top tip:

Many SENCOs use public social media platforms to problem-solve. These can be anonymous or named. I find it fascinating reading 'how' SENCOs frame the problem. This impacts the type of responses they receive, and in some cases, misinformation. Consider 'how' you frame problems and what impact this has on finding answers.

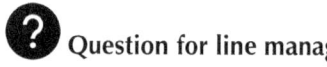Question for line managers:

If SENCOs are relying on social media platforms for advice to solve their problems, how are they discerning good advice from poor advice or even conflicting ideas of support? Such platforms contain both experienced and inexperienced SENCOs and the tone of response (especially wit and sarcasm) could be misinterpreted. (More on this in Chapter 14.)

Further reading:

Leadbeater, C. (2016). The problem solvers, Pearson [pdf download]. https://www.pearson.com/content/dam/corporate/global/pearson-dot-com/files/learning/Problem-Solvers-Web-.pdf

DIMENSION 2: LEADERSHIP SKILLS

## 2. Effective communication

**What is this?** SENCOs communicate using four main methods:

a) Written
b) Verbal
c) Presentations
d) Meetings

Each requires a distinctive approach depending on the audience and the purpose. Given the legal ramifications of the SENCO role, it is important to strike a balance and clarity between facts, opinions and assumptions.

**Why does it matter?** Leadership is about being relational. A SENCO is interacting with seven people groups (SEND7). This includes themselves! However, back to identity and the transition from teacher to SENCO, the crux of effective teaching is communicating attitudes to learning, skills and knowledge to a diverse audience (e.g. a class of 30). Being a teacher involves writing reports and presenting to/meeting with parents.

Communication is an area, where I think SENCOs are not given enough training and support. Styles and approaches to language change over time. At this point in time (2024), it is possible to have five different generations in schools from Boomers (born 1946–1965) to Alpha (born 2011–2025). Imagine all the different communication styles used by all five groups (Boomers, Gen X, Gen Y Millennials, Gen Z, Alpha). Some of the communication differentials will be driven by access (or not) to technology, at different points in time.

There are strategies SENCOs can employ to support their development in this area.

**Written communication:** Always ask someone to proofread. Automated spell checkers do not always work. To cite an example, A SEND communication was sent out to parents of children with hearing impairment. Instead of the word 'deaf', the word 'death' was inserted. This took a lot of follow-up communications to resolve. Many parents naturally were distressed by this mass communication using such insensitive language. It was a genuine error, but once sent out, it cannot be easily recalled. With quick replies to emails these days and messaging, sometimes the tone of intent is lost.

**Verbal:** Rehearse. It sounds so basic, but modern technology now affords us the opportunity to video ourselves or audio record. So, we can check tone, emphasis, body language, eye contact and posture. All these non-verbal cues make a difference.

As a SENCO, I have previously asked colleagues to sit in on verbal communication situations with me and their task is not to engage, but after the discussion provide me with feedback. I'm interested in what I did well, but more importantly what I could do better and how.

**Presentations:** This can be with visual aids or without. Defining the key message in a presentation is vital. Experienced speakers would also encourage you to consider using the 'Power of 3'. Things to avoid include reading from the screen, not connecting with the audience and using monotone throughout.

**Meetings:** I've written elsewhere (Devi & Bowers, 2022) about SENCOs not just focusing on the agenda of a meeting, but also the purpose. Fundamentally, a meeting serves three purposes – gathering information, disseminating information or joint problem-solving. Are you clear on the purpose of the meeting and is this communicated to all involved?

Whichever method of communication is used, underpinning all of them is the power of persuasion. In Chapter 2, I referred to ethos, pathos and logos. Every effective communication will contain a combination of these.

**Action task:** Having read the above and researched the power of persuasion, redraft a communication you have already written, sent or shared. What would you change or do differently and what desired effect would this result in?

## 3. Conflict management

No one intentionally comes into the SENCO role to resolve differences of opinion. Different motivational factors have already been addressed in Part 1. Most embark on the SENCO career wanting to make a difference (internally in the setting or in the wider profession) (Douglas & Dobson 2020a, 2020b). Yet conflict is a natural part of the SEND arena, not because there is a lack of trust (Lamb, 2009), but because seven different people groups are looking at the same situation from seven or more different perspectives. So, conflict, difference and difficult conversations are to be expected. This is rarely discussed at the time of recruitment or in the induction programme.

SENCOs arrive fresh in the role, with aspirations for themselves and others and the disparity of what they see in results is a reality shock (Yih, 2021). This shock is disguised loss, from their envisaged imagination of 'what could be' to accepting 'what is'. With this loss comes grief. Some SENCOs handle it better than others. I would suggest, those secure in their identity as teachers and/or leaders handle it better. This is why defining steps along the career trajectory (Chapter 7) is important.

**What is this?** Conflict management is the ability to accept difference and then using their own values and skills navigate all parties to a common agreement or consensus. Conflict management requires self-awareness and sensitivity towards others. It is not about being a SENCO who is a people pleaser (Devi & Bowers, 2022).

**Why does it matter?** Without harnessing the ability to step back from a conflict, SENCOs either end up trying to please everyone or pleasing no one. The emotional drain of both these extreme states on a regular basis is taxing and can lead to compassion fatigue (see Chapter 5). However, where SENCOs have created processes for themselves for resolving conflict, there appears to be less tension, even if not all stakeholders get what they want.

Investing in SENCO wellbeing regularly is vital here. Conflict situations cannot be personalised, and yet they often 'feel' personal. It is easy for a SENCO to feel they are failing when conflict arises. However, knowing that conflict is inevitable and manageable helps SENCOs deal with situations from a learning perspective. Denial, on the other hand, can lead to escalation.

**Further reading:**

Devi, A., & Bowers, J. (2022). *Journeying to the heart of SENCO wellbeing*. London: Routledge.

**Further training:**

Accredited course – Managing Difficult Conversations in Education by TeamADL (www.teamadl.uk).

## 4. Team management

**What is this?** Personal qualities/attributes and being appointed to a position are only two-thirds of the leader triad. The third dimension is followers. A leader is defined by those who follow and the formation of teams.

**Action task:**

Watch this three-minute video – Leadership Lessons from Dancing Guy (https://www.youtube.com/watch?v=fW8amMCVAJQ).

**Why does it matter?** If leadership is about driving change, then knowing who your followers and allies are, is critical for implementing anything new. Within any team, following takes time and with the SEND7, I would argue that the SENCO leads the largest team in educational settings, yet it is the best-kept secret! Most refer to support staff as the SENCO's team. But go back and read Regulation 50 in Chapter 1 – a SENCO's team is very broad!

**Myth busting:**

From the mouths of SENCOs: 'Everyone should do exactly what I tell them to do!' Not true, essentially, it is about winning people over to come on your vision journey (see Chapter 6).

Nurturing followers and building teams isn't an instant process. Nor is it automatic because a SENCO has been given a title. These things happen over time and there has to be both persistence and consistency in relationships and team building.

### Self-audit grid for discussions with line managers

Table 9.1 presents each of the four dimensions of leadership skills, building in capacity for growth if circumstances change, year on year. In Chapter 14, I provide a case study example of how this could be used with the other six dimensions of SLIM (Devi, 2022).

Read through the descriptors along the rows and *choose the best fit for this moment in time*. There is no right or wrong answer. It is about knowing where the SENCO currently is and what the potential for growth is.

Once the SENCO has completed this, I would suggest talking through the self-audit with their line manager. In particular, asking if they agree and jointly considering what evidence would support the best-fit judgement.

The discussion should raise further discussion points, such as what are the opportunities for growth? What further support is required? Does the SENCO exhibit a high level of leadership behaviours in an outside setting and is there potential for transference to school?

## DIMENSION 2: LEADERSHIP SKILLS

Table 9.1 Five level descriptors for segments of the leadership skills dimension (Devi, 2022)

| | 1<br>Aware | 2<br>Learning | 3<br>Know | 4<br>Apply | 5<br>Confident |
|---|---|---|---|---|---|
| Problem-solving | I am aware of current problems but am unclear on how to resolve them. | I am beginning to research three to five different approaches to problem-solving. | I know the similarities and differences between different approaches to solving problems and can choose suitable ones depending on the context/situation. | I can apply (with support) my chosen problem-solving strategy to a specific situation. | I am confident in using a range of problem-solving strategies and can be agile between them. |
| Effective communication | I recognise I have strengths in communication, and I am aware people have preferences for receiving different types of information in specific ways. These do not always match up. | I am intentionally trying to find out which methods work best with different agents in the SEND7. This includes methods of communicating and timing. | I know the best times and approaches to use when communicating different types of information to different people. | I am applying different approaches and methods to communication to make information sharing more streamlined and succinct. I am getting better at reflecting and refining my communications. | I am confident in switching between different modes of communication to different people considering the purpose of the communication and the intended impact I want the two-way interaction to have. |

*(Continued)*

Table 9.1 (Continued)

| | 1 Aware | 2 Learning | 3 Know | 4 Apply | 5 Confident |
|---|---|---|---|---|---|
| Conflict management | I avoid managing conflicts until I absolutely have to. | I am learning to pick my battles and where I make a mistake take ownership of the learning by talking it through with someone. | I know at least three to five strategies for managing conflict and dealing with difficult conversations. | I am versatile in applying different approaches to managing conflict. | I confidently walk into potential conflict situations and facilitate a way through, leaving all parties feeling they have contributed and have been heard. |
| Team management | I manage a micro team within the wider setting. | I am learning to build connections with the wider team and SEND7 – sharing my knowledge and expertise and learning from their ideas too. | I know the strengths of all team members (across SEND7), as well as how to keep them motivated and engaged. | I am applying different strategies to grow and strengthen a bigger team, so that all know and feel they can contribute to the inclusion agenda. | I am confident in calling on different members of the wider team to take the lead on different aspects. I trust their communication and judgement. I make myself available to coach them if they need it. |

SLIM (Devi, 2022): Leadership skills: *Connected leadership (distributed power)*

DIMENSION 2: LEADERSHIP SKILLS

 **Question:**

What are your top three takeaways from this chapter?

## Summary

This chapter considered why leadership skills matter and how this impacts SENCOs in the way they communicate, find solutions to problems, build teams and resolve conflict.

Chapter 10 focuses on critical thinking skills and unpacks four specific skill sets SENCOS need to develop.

PART 2

# 10 | Dimension 3: Critical thinking skills

*The role of SENCO involves the use of multiple forms of data, often conflicting. Demonstrating an ability to analyse, reason and synthesise is vital to being successful, and more importantly, the accurate identification of the needs of children and young people.*

As part of my career journey, I led and delivered the MA in inclusive education (which is 180 credits at level 7). At other higher education institutions (HEIs), I delivered guest lectures to SENCOs completing their NASENCO, and for one establishment, I was (for four years) the external examiner of the NASENCO Post Graduate Certificate (PGCert) in Education. The NASENCO was 60 credits of a master's degree. One of my observations from leading, teaching and examining level 7 courses was that students developed critical thinking skills by engaging with academic literature and research. It was something they wrestled with for the first 120 credits, having been introduced to these higher-order thinking skills and learning the difference between criticism and critical thinking. But on completion of their master's degree, they got it! What is it? Tacit knowledge, i.e. the knowledge, skills and abilities an individual gains through experience that is often difficult to put into words or otherwise communicate but is rooted in context, experience, practice and values.

For SENCOs, I believe this was a critical development for their internal schema to think like SENCOs. Thought is a forerunner to action. So, if SENCOs think like SENCOs, they will act like SENCO leaders.

Examining case-based cognitive skills in leaders, Mumford et al. (2017) identified nine critical thinking skills as a determinant of leader performance. In my research, SENCOs identified four key critical skills that map onto the nine identified by Mumford et al. (2017). These are:

- Questioning skills
- Reasoning
- Analysis
- Synthesis

All four combined create the ability to both deconstruct and reconstruct diverse data to create a meaningful structure.

## DIMENSION 3: CRITICAL THINKING SKILLS

 **Reminder:**

**Connected leadership** embraces emotional capital, shared vision and purpose, and a focus on building relationships, not just maintaining them (Tian et al., 2016).

Critical thinking skills relate to connected leadership approaches. Therefore, both internally and externally, the SENCO is 'joining the dots' at three levels – the data, the people (SEND7, who all contribute different forms of data) and actions (what next steps). The connecting people element and actions help to imbibe 'distributed power' (Tian et al., 2016). Basically, this is the notion that it takes an inclusive way of working to create an environment of inclusion.

**Legislation:**

*Quoting from the SEND Code of Practice (Department for Education, 2015) pages 93, 94, 100, 105:*

> **6.4** The quality of teaching for pupils with SEN, and the progress made by pupils, should be a core part of the school's performance management arrangements and its approach to professional development for all teaching and support staff. **School leaders and teaching staff, including the SENCO, should identify any patterns in the identification of SEN, both within the school and in comparison, with national data, and use these to reflect on and reinforce the quality of teaching.**
>
> **6.5** The identification of SEN should be **built into the overall approach** to monitoring the progress and development of all pupils.
>
> ...
>
> **6.14** All schools should have a clear approach to identifying and responding to SEN. The benefits of early identification are widely recognised – identifying need at the earliest point and then making effective provision improves long-term outcomes for the child or young person.
>
> ...
>
> **6.27** These four broad areas give an overview of the range of needs that should be planned for. The purpose of identification is to work out what action the school needs to take, not to fit a pupil into a category.
>
> ...
>
> **6.45** In identifying a child as needing SEN support **the class or subject teacher, working with the SENCO**, should carry out a clear analysis of the pupil's needs. This should draw on the teacher's assessment and experience of the pupil, their previous progress and attainment, as well as information from the school's core approach to pupil progress, attainment, and behaviour. It should also draw on other subject teachers' assessments where relevant,

the individual's development in comparison to their peers and national data, the views and experience of parents, the pupil's own views and, if relevant, advice from external support services. Schools should take seriously any concerns raised by a parent. These should be recorded and compared to the setting's own assessment and information on how the pupil is developing.

...

**6.77** Provision management can be used strategically to develop special educational provision to match the assessed needs of pupils across the school, and to evaluate the impact of that provision on pupil progress. Used in this way provision management can also contribute to school improvement by identifying particular patterns of need and potential areas of development for teaching staff. It can help the school to develop the use of interventions that are effective and to remove those that are less so. It can support schools to improve their core offer for all pupils as the most effective approaches are adopted more widely across the school.

> It takes an inclusive way of working to create an environment of inclusion.

From the above, it can be seen that critical thinking is a core skill that *SENCOs need to continually develop and also pass on to others.*

 **Question:**

When was the last time you or a SENCO led training for staff on critical thinking skills for supporting SEND?

 **Action task:**

Before reading any further, take the four crucial thinking skills identified by SENCOS and record what you think they mean in the context of being a SENCO, plus examples you already see in your setting (Table 10.1).

*Table 10.1* Reflection: What do the four subdimensions of critical thinking skills mean to me

|  | How would I define this? | Where have I seen this in my setting in relation to SEND? | What could be even better? |
|---|---|---|---|
| Questioning skills |  |  |  |
| Reasoning |  |  |  |
| Analysis |  |  |  |
| Synthesis |  |  |  |

# DIMENSION 3: CRITICAL THINKING SKILLS

## 1. Questioning

This is a core skill used in the classroom by teachers to elicit information, stretch thinking and generate new ideas. The same applies to being a SENCO. The most effective teachers in the classroom know how to use a range of different questioning techniques, erring more towards open questions, where there isn't a single right answer. Some teachers in the classroom often flip the dialogue, stating, 'This is the answer, so what is the question?' If all of these are embedded in a SENCO's identity and agency as a classroom practitioner, applying this to the SEND context becomes a smooth transition.

Action task:

Look back at Chapters 3 and 4.

**What is this?** A repertoire of articulated phrases to elicit vital information from others and see patterns in any data gathered. Questioning skills is about asking oneself (internal reflections) and others (external conversations), as well as reconciling the two. In terms of interpersonal skills, questioning skills can act as relationship foundation blocks for deepening understanding and gaining different perspectives. From an individual perspective, it requires a heightened level of self-awareness.

**Why does it matter?** In the context of SEND, questioning skills help to ensure problem definition, goal determination and implemented provision are agreed upon by different stakeholders of SEND7.

*I'm not afraid to ask questions.*
– SENCO I8

*Probably like many jobs it's one of those where you might have a problem and there's not a right answer to solve it.*
– SENCO I27

In England, in relation to providing SEND provision for children and young people, the governing bodies of schools give the SENCO delegated powers to lead the day-to-day operations of SENCOs. Young (2016) considers asking the right questions in relation to governing bodies. Using non-participation observation methodology, Young (2016) raises the question of whether 'prescribed criticality' is operating in schools, i.e. training provided determines and shapes what questions are asked. The NASENCO was originally set at level 7, I believe, to ensure SENCOs develop their skills around critical thinking. I have no doubt this is what providers seek to deliver (Passy et al., 2017). However, I would question how explicitly this is delivered and whether the transference of the 'study' process from the induction qualification is applied to the SENCO role. Or is it perceived as a threshold to simply pass? At present, the induction qualification does not consider accredited prior learning (APL) as part of its assessment process. The question, therefore, remains, would APL enhance the transference of skills both in terms of pedagogical practice and leadership?

## 2. Reasoning

**What is this?** Adopting a chain of logic to discern possible causes and possible solutions.

Let me explain this with an example.

> **Teacher to SENCO:** Abdul has a problem with writing.

This doesn't actually tell the SENCO very much. However, by adopting a framework across the four broad areas of need, the SENCO can look for other supporting data. A reasoning schema of inquiry for Abdul might look like Figure 10.1.

The SENCO would then explore other data and/or put interventions in place to notice 'what is working'. Elsewhere (Devi, 2020), I have expanded on each of the four areas of need.

### *Why does it matter?*

Reasoning was recognised as vital to necessitate barriers and plan the next steps. Pinnock and Welch (2014) argue that clinical reasoning is the product of supervised practice and effective feedback. Admittedly, SENCOs are not clinicians. SENCOs are involved in the identification of special educational needs, but not (necessarily) disability. All the SENCOs in my research reported they have no supervision, and many commented on poor line management, 'I've been left to my own devices really' (SENCO I12) and 'My line manager doesn't know really what my job is' (SENCO I21). This raises the question of how SENCOs are checking out their reasoning skills for the identification and implementation of provision. In relation to CPD choices, SENCOs in the questionnaire element of my research indicated they preferred face-to-face meetings and online communities of practice. The challenge with both being the sector and organisational element of the conceptual framework (see Chapter 6) varies from setting to setting (Tissot, 2013), and without a progressive pathway for SENCOs, expertise is defined by the number of years in post, as opposed to a more tangible structure for consulting those more experienced and whose work has been quality assured.

> *I am curious about what works.*
> – SENCO I9 [… therefore by default, what's not working].

Questioning skills and reasoning work in tandem with analysis to ensure the situation and what's required are correctly identified.

DIMENSION 3: CRITICAL THINKING SKILLS

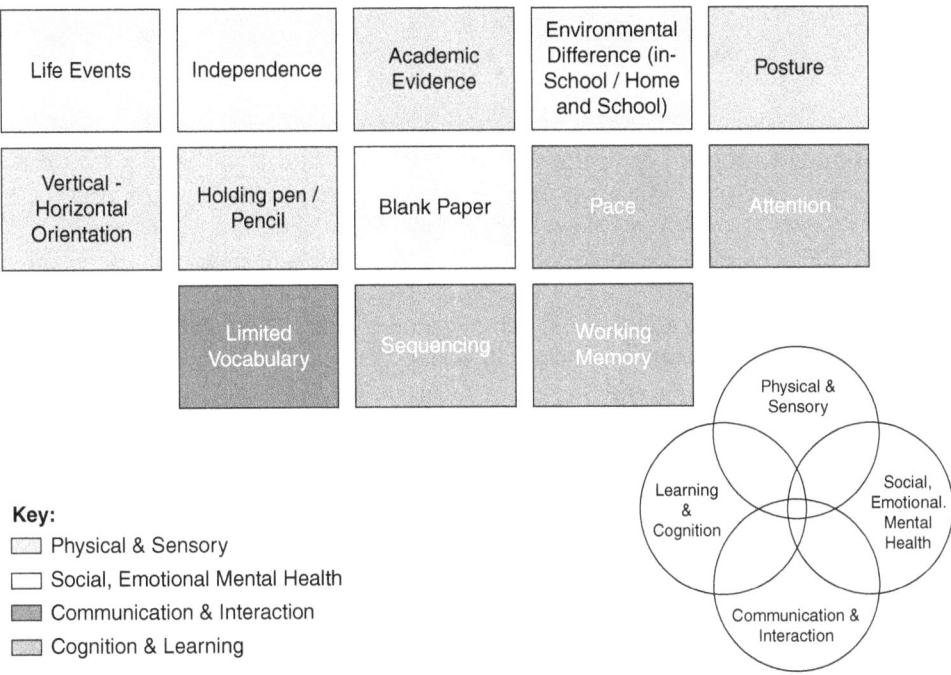

*Figure 10.1* Thirteen reasons why Abdul has a problem with writing across the four broad areas of need

## 3. Analysis

**What is this?** Analysis involves the determined and detailed examination of the elements or structure of special educational needs presenting in different children and young people.

Reconsider Figure 10.1. What if the teacher provided additional information such as Abdul has historically had a low attendance record and he can be quite uncoordinated in physical education (PE)? These two pieces of information bring together social context and a developmental aspect of Abdul's physicality. Is there a connection between the two? Sometimes there is and sometimes there is not. It is this level of analysis a SENCO is required to pursue. The line of inquiry would be different if the teacher reported, 'Abdul finds it difficult to concentrate and follow more than two step instructions'.

**Why does it matter?** Analysis affords a SENCO the framework to look at detail, whilst also keeping a view on the development of the whole child. This micro/macro understanding is vital for synthesis.

> *I always consider and I always reflect on the different leaders I've had. Whether they've been visionary or mentoring or you know. So, I think I take the elements, I think worked that I worked well under and try to implement all those things into how I lead.*
> – SENCO I16

Dobson and Douglas (2020a) identify the different drivers that motivate a teacher to apply for a SENCO role. Depending on whether the determinants are microsystems (i.e. direct experiences), mesosystems (i.e. aspirational for involvement and change), exosystems (i.e. driving change) or macrosystems (i.e. shaping the wider system) (Anderson et al., 2014; Dobson & Douglas, 2020a), this can impact a SENCO's engagement with analysing the data. The lens of motivation in the individual aspect identified in the conceptual framework of my research (see Chapter 6) does affect where their focus is directed. Whilst the induction qualification may cover personal motivations at the time of induction, these change over time. Therefore, highlighting this skill within a broader pathway of growth provides SENCOs with opportunities to continually reflect on who they are (identity) and why they are doing what they are doing (agency).

Data analysis is only one side of the coin, and given that the data in SEND can be varied and from different stakeholders, synthesising conflicting data was viewed by SENCOs in this study as an important skill.

> *I'm developing my ability to question, challenge other professionals. That's been quite difficult.*
> – SENCO I21

### 4. Synthesis

As the needs of children and young people increase (DfE, 2024), as well as the complexity of needs now in mainstream schools, due to the lack of special school places (National Audit Office, 2019), SENCOs will need to continually enhance their skills to synthesise diverse and conflicting data. Whether special schools are the answer or not is a philosophical debate on inclusion and wider aspects of sector and organisation (as identified in the conceptual framework). These are areas beyond their direct control (Covery, 2004). Through the development of these skill sets, SENCOs are enhancing their individual identity within the framework to become 'agents of change' (Dobson & Douglas, 2020a, 2020b). Synthesis is a skill vital for knowing what it is that they can change to have the biggest impact (agency).

**What is this?** Creating a connected whole picture of the child and young person's needs across the four broad areas of need and education, health and social care, as well as a connected view of the setting provision. This is why a provision framework matters, yet it was omitted in the 2014 Children and Families Act – see Chapter 8.

**Why does it matter?** Synthesis becomes the substantive framework for relationships and growth. It communicates to SEND7 that you have been heard, your perspective has

# DIMENSION 3: CRITICAL THINKING SKILLS

informed actions and your responsible contribution matters. If done well, it can bring together broad-ranging views. If managed ineffectively, it can be divisive.

A useful template for the 4 × 3 schema at the individual child/young person level could be the arrangement presented in Table 10.2.

At the whole school level, the SENCO needs to hold in place micro elements of the day-to-day plus wider strategic aims for improvement, as well as managing a change process for capacity building (Figure 10.2).

This is where a SENCO time management framework becomes imperative (see the Further Reading list at the end of this chapter and Chapter 14).

## Self-audit grid for discussions with line managers

Table 10.3 presents each of the four dimensions of critical thinking skills. In Chapter 14, I provide a case study example of how this could be used with the other six dimensions of SLIM (Devi, 2022).

*Table 10.2* Reflection: Four broad areas of need across education, health and social care

|  | Education | Health | Social Care |
|---|---|---|---|
| Physical and sensory<br>Social, emotional mental health<br>Communication and interaction<br>Cognition and learning |  |  |  |

Note the order the four broad areas of need are listed in.

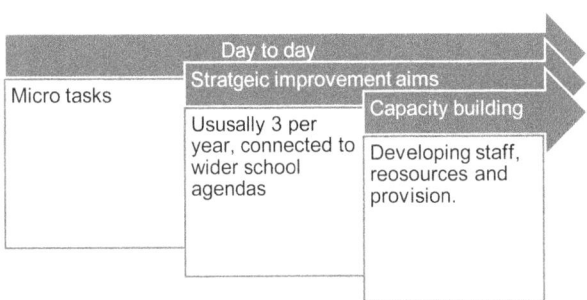

*Figure 10.2* Synthesising leadership elements of the role

Table 10.3 Five level descriptors for segments of the critical thinking skills dimensions (Devi, 2022)

| | 1 Aware | 2 Learning | 3 Know | 4 Apply | 5 Confident |
|---|---|---|---|---|---|
| Questioning | I tend to provide all the answers, believing I am the one who should know and do it all. Most of the questions I ask others are closed, thereby eliciting a specific answer that I want to hear. | I am learning to ask questions and reflect on any problems that arise. I am learning to make myself available to be asked questions, particularly open-ended ones. | I know at least three to five approaches to asking open questions of my wider team and giving them time and space to respond. This transforms our interactions into a two-way dialogue. | I am applying a range of questioning strategies, thereby adopting a more coaching approach to working with others and developing them as practitioners. | I am confident in using a person-centred approach to my leadership by asking different types of questions in different contexts. I am comfortable when people ask questions of me, even when I do not have the answer. |
| Reasoning | I tend to react most of the time. Striving is my default. Most of the time, it is just about getting through the day. | I am learning to make time to think and both reflect back and project forward. I am seeking to learn to thrive. | I know my optimal times for thinking and the best approaches to use. I know I am beginning to flourish. | I am applying the reasoning that evolves from my thinking time to solving problems, communicating with others and training colleagues. | I can confidently think through a problem/situation, reason it out and then communicate my rationale to others, whilst also listening to their reasoning. |

(Continued)

Table 10.3 (Continued)

|  | 1 Aware | 2 Learning | 3 Know | 4 Apply | 5 Confident |
|---|---|---|---|---|---|
| Analysis | I find handling data tricky and rarely ask questions to see any patterns. | I am learning to examine data by asking questions about what I can see, as well as what I cannot see. | I know how to not only present my analysis to others but also explain the process behind it. | I am applying data analysis methods (quantitative and qualitative) to a range of different contexts and situations. | I am confident in analysing data, asking questions about the data and making deductions and inferences from the data. |
| Synthesis | I rarely bring different data sources together to create an informed perspective of the situation. | I am learning to appreciate the value of conflicting data to draw out further questions of inquiry. | I know how to combine multiple and often conflicting forms of data sets to create a coherent approach for defining the next steps. | I am applying my ability to synthesise data to both individual cases, as well as wider strategic development areas. | I am confident at presenting multiple and often conflicting data sets to a wider range of audiences, helping them to draw inferences and deductions from the information I present. |

SLIM (Devi, 2022): Critical thinking skills: *Connected leadership (distributed power)*

Read through the descriptors along the rows in Table 10.3 and *choose the best fit for this moment in time*. There is no right or wrong answer. It is about knowing where the SENCO currently is and what the potential for growth is.

Once the SENCO has completed this, I would suggest talking through the self-audit with their line manager. In particular, asking if they agree and jointly considering what evidence would support the best-fit judgement.

The discussion should raise further discussion points, such as what are the opportunities for growth or further development.

Further reading:

Devi, A. (2016). *Take time – time management strategies and case studies for SENCOs* [eBook]. London: Optimus Publishing.
Devi, A. (2020). (Series Editor Hollis, E.) *Essential guides for early career teachers: Special educational needs and disability.* London: Critical Publishing.
Devi, A., & Jagger, S. (2025). *Neuroplasticity and neurodiversity in the classroom.* London: Critical Publishing.

Further training:

SEND in the Classroom (2022) Accredited Course on the Four Areas of Need by High Speed Training.

**?** Question:

What are your top three takeaways from this chapter?

## Summary

This chapter has highlighted the importance of critical thinking skills in relation to the job description and workload of a SENCO. Not always considered, but being effective in this area helps to build strong relationships amongst the SEND7.

Chapter 11 highlights the power and potential of strong interpersonal skills.

PART 2

# 11 | Dimension 4: Interpersonal skills

*Building a team, leading a team and relating to team members are three distinctive skill sets. This chapter looks at micro-behaviours within teams. It is clear from the research that SENCOs were able to recognise the importance of relationships and listening skills (Green, 2016) in defining their identity. However, they rarely invested time in this and/or used it as a catalytic driver for efficiency.*

Authentic leadership influences both performance and team reflexivity (Lyubovnikova et al., 2017). SENCOs (from my research and observations from my working practice) highlight that SENCOs do not appear to have fully grasped the construct of teams (Solberg et al., 2021) as essential for the leadership of inclusion and that leadership is distinct from being called a leader. This is not intended as a criticism of individuals, but more of a reflection of how the cultural shift of the SEND Reforms (2010–2018) has not been actualised. Prior to the changes in 2014, the responsibility of SEN fell on the SENCO. The SEND Reforms sought to change this, making it everyone's responsibility (see Chapter 9). In effect, the aspiration was the SENCO went from co-ordinating to leading. However:

- The title did not change; it could have gone from SENCO → SEND leader.
- Working practices and systems did not evolve to consider distributed leadership models (Tian et al., 2016).
- No new frameworks were implemented to combine SEN + D (Castro & Palikara, 2016).
- Nor was a career trajectory or leadership model constructed to support SENCOs (Devi, 2022).

In effect, a lot of SENCOs invest time doing the day-to-day (operational) role whilst trying to raise their influence through status to become more strategic, if they had the time! Yet, instead, if they were to build teams, the day-to-day work would be shared and their influence would widen. I've already discussed at length (Chapter 7) that simply placing a SENCO on the SLT does not change the ways of working. As a long-standing SEND consultant, I am mostly called in to support schools or colleges that are in a difficult place. Here's how some of the conversations go:

**Me to SLT:** How would you define the SEND team?
**SLT Member:** Well, we have a department and a number of teaching assistants.

**Me to teacher:** Who would you say is on the SEND team?
**Teacher:** The support staff and SENCO.

**Me to SENCO:** Tell me about your team.
**SENCO:** I have five teaching assistants, some part-time. We are struggling to recruit teaching assistants.

*Now consider the dialogue, where I have been or am currently a part-time (PT) SENCO:*
**Inspector:** Tell me about the SEND team.
**Me:** Everyone is on the team. We have clearly articulated everyone's role and our expectations for their contribution. My teachers make the biggest contribution to meeting needs. They plan lessons well and direct our support staff effectively.

> I should add that in many of the settings I work with/or at, we have an annual expectation that all staff read at least chapters 1 and 6 of the SENDCoP 2015 every year in the autumn term and they have to sign a document to say they have! (Some schools add in Chapter 5 for early years and Chapter 7 for secondary/colleges.)

**Me to the Inspector:** (and before they ask) Can I share with you our record that shows staff have read two critical chapters of SEND CoP 2015 every year? Can I give you a copy of the 'Provision for All' document we create annually with the SEND7? This sets out our expectations for all students and staff. It's just two pages long and you could use it in class as you visit different lessons.

 **Question:**

How do you think this goes down with the Inspectorate?

[NB: The two-page Provision for All document is based on a SEND Review methodology developed by TeamADL and many inspectors have found it useful to recognise good practice during an inspection.]

As part of the research, SENCOs were invited to reflect on the narrative of influence (to date) on their leadership identity. SENCOS were asked to share with three key people some anecdotes or experiences that had impacted them. This was relevant, as it formed part of the conceptual framework structure (see Chapter 6). Figure 11.1 was provided for them to generate their responses.

In describing narratives about who or what had influenced their leadership, SENCOs shared they learnt equally from good role models/experiences, as well as those they considered to be ineffective/challenging. The focus, in most cases, however, was on the 'individual' leading, not the team or purpose for which they were leading. What was also

DIMENSION 4: INTERPERSONAL SKILLS

# Leadership: your journey

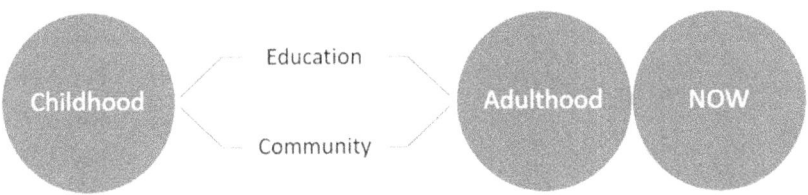

*Figure 11.1* Stimulus used during interviews for SENCOs to articulate three key episodes in their leadership formation

useful to note was if given the right structure, SENCOs (in terms of their leadership) could be reflective, reflexive and teachable.

> **Reflection:** Looking back on encounters and experiences to highlight salient points for growth.
> **Reflexive:** Able to internalise the impact of encounters and experiences on themselves to raise self-awareness of both contributions and experiencing the consequences.
> **Feedback:** Gathering information from different people about performance and areas for growth.
> **Teachable:** An individual open to learning from reflection, reflexive thinking and feedback.

> *I think in childhood, it might be worth mentioning I'm the second child of five. So, I've always been a deputy leader. So, after the brave courageous charge of number one, then I sometimes had to smooth over some of the more difficulties that were caused by that ... The one in adulthood, it was a real eye-opener for me. The first school I taught in; they had this headteacher who had this fabulously, it wasn't collaborative, but it was just his way of leading, he managed to bring everybody on board. To the extent where we didn't bother paying the insurance for sick leave because nobody went off sick.*
> – SENCO 19

> *I think my mum probably, was the best leader I could think of. I mean she had five kids all one year after another and that was some serious leadership going on there. Keeping us all in control and none of us ever got into trouble and she could take any of us out at any point ... But I have recently, sadly, had the experience of really bad leadership ... within a school. And actually, seeing what bad leadership can really impact and how it can tear down a school in a matter of months. And that's really sad to see, the devastation that bad leadership can really have. And although you hear it and you speak about it, and in the courses, you*

*hear all about good and bad leadership. But actually, seeing the impact of bad leadership on a school that you absolutely love, it's quite devastating, it's quite heart-breaking. And then to hear that they've then gone into school improvement which is just terrifying.*

*– SENCO I7*

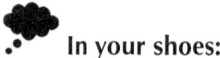 **In your shoes:**

When was the last time the SENCO appraisal included conversations around reflections, reflexivity, purposeful feedback or teachability?

Previously, SENCOs had to mainly consider the SLT of a setting in terms of leadership influence. Under the academisation journey, there is the localised SLT, MAT leadership and (for some) SEND MAT Central Team leads in addition to local authority SEND personnel (Figure 11.2). Just as the culture of each school differs, so do MATs. This by and large is led by both the ethos and size of the MAT. For example, some MATs have a standardised approach across all schools. So, a top-down hierarchy is promoted in the wider educational community, whilst the SENCO is aiming to develop a distributed leadership approach to SEND within the school. In other MATs, each school is encouraged to develop their own individuality within a wider group framework. Many of the dynamics also change as the MAT evolves by acquiring and/or losing schools. Many MAT CEOs talk of developing collaborating relationships with neighbouring MATs, yet the reality is there is also a competitive edge. Some might argue the sector (see Chapter 6) is in a state of Co-opetition (von Neumann, 1944; Copeland, 1945). In other words, there is co-operative competition. This is now another layer to the postcode lottery of accessing different provisions to support SEND.

When we constructed the SEND7 concept (Devi & Bowers, 2022, p. 36), we intentionally left out the possibility of multiple academy trusts, as we focused on the geographical

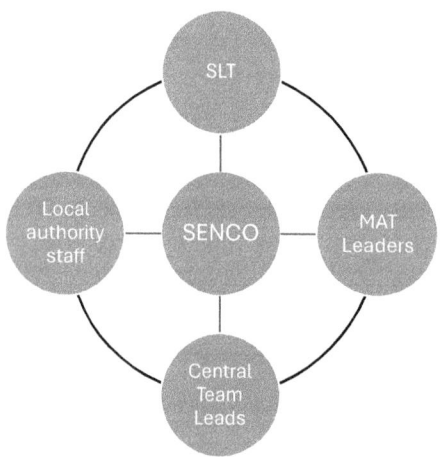

*Figure 11.2* Leadership influences for the SENCO under academisation

DIMENSION 4: INTERPERSONAL SKILLS

proximity of seven schools in an imaginary place called 'Inclusion Ville'. However, as academisation accelerates, it's possible for some schools that SEND7 will become SEND8 with the eighth group being Central Teams in a MAT. And so, the team the SENCO co-ordinates continues to grow!

 **Action task:**

visit www.inclusionville.me

Interpersonal skills as a dimension of SLIM (Devi, 2022) reflects the 'building relationships' element of connected leadership, as such, it can be deconstructed into four elements:

1. Active listening
2. Supporting teams
3. Stretching colleagues
4. Motivating self and others

 **Reminder:**

**Connected leadership** embraces emotional capital, shared vision and purpose, and a focus on building relationships, not just maintaining them (Tian et al., 2016).

## 1. Active listening

*Everyone listens, but not everyone hears.*

**What is this?** Active listening therefore is listening to understand another perspective, not their thoughts within your own framework. It requires intentionality, presence and stillness. Often, many of us in everyday conversation 'listen to respond',

> Listening is not just understanding the words of the question asked. Listening is understanding why the question was asked in the first place.
>
> – Simon Sinek

 **Action task:**

Look up Sinek's art of listening videos on YouTube.

109

**Why does it matter?** SENCOs are not expected to have all the answers! The title implies co-ordinating. Who and what are SENCOs co-ordinating?

1. Different people groups
2. Different needs
3. Different views
4. Different circumstances
5. Different datasets
6. Different provisions
7. Different seasons

> If SENCOs were to build teams, the day-to-day work would be shared, and their influence would widen.

This last one tends to make SENCOs ask, 'Seasons?' We have termly rotation and an annual calendar (see Chapter 1) but there are also seasons within communities and for the individual. Looking back over my SENCO career, when I first arrived at the school, the season was very much about fact-finding. I did a lot of listening! This informed the next season for me, which was about envisioning. This was followed by planting seeds … this took time and more listening. Eventually, the season of growth began. This was slow and painful … everyone on the SEND7 team was growing at a different pace.

I relish meeting new SENCOs, and one thing I hear more often than I want to, 'I need to change everything like yesterday!' That tells me, they are not listening, but doing! Listening builds teams because people experience a sense of belonging.

Each month, I lead my team to write an inclusion blog. We've spent a lot of time debating what inclusion actually means to us. We eventually narrowed it down to:

*Being | Belonging | Becoming*

Investing time in this shared understanding has helped us grow exponentially because everything comes back to these three facets of inclusion.

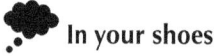 **In your shoes:**

Who in your SEND7 needs to be heard more?

A friend and former police officer at Scotland Yard, Nicky Perfelct, often states it as 'Everyone talks, some hear, few listen, Almost no-one understands'. This reminds me of the *Everybody, Somebody, Anybody and Nobody story* I shared in Chapter 9.

DIMENSION 4: INTERPERSONAL SKILLS

## 2. Supporting teams

*A question I always ask SENCOs – Do the SEND7 know they are on your team?*

**What is this?** Whilst active listening is about the SENCO receiving information, supporting teams is about giving to others. This requires SENCOs to know their team members, know where they are at and what they need. Across seven people groups, that's a lot. However, if the active listening is structured and systematic, then the supporting naturally follows.

**Why does it matter?** Support accelerates growth and participation. If, as a SENCO, you want others to take on more responsibility, you have to create the scaffolds for that to happen.

> Scaffolding in education is a term coined by Vygotsky (1896–1934) to connect what an individual can do without help and what he or she can achieve with guidance and encouragement from a skilled partner (i.e. the SENCO). Simply giving someone information doesn't necessarily mean they will know how to use that information in an effective way to improve practice.

**Action task:**

This is a CPD activity I've often led with staff at the beginning of the year.

> **Materials needed:** Origami t-shirts made from A4 paper or a 2D cut-out t-shirt shape. Sports teams take great pride in their t-shirts. It can also tell them about their role on the team (e.g. striker, goalkeeper, defence) Often, a memorable event/activity will have a branded t-shirt.
>
> **Activity:** Ask team members to put a number on the *back* and a personal identifier. They can also add the words 'Team SEND'. On the *front*, ask team members to write down what it is they bring to the team: skills, attributes, experience, knowledge etc.
>
> **Discussion:** What have people added to the front? Can they think of any more?
>
> **Follow-up:** Hang up the t-shirts so they remind everyone – they all have something to contribute.
>
> *You have to build a team to support a team.*

### 3. Stretching colleagues

**What is this?** This is the belief that team members can and want to do better. This isn't always about doing more, but more often than not about doing differently.

**Why does it matter?** After the invitation to be on the team, comes the challenge. Challenge is received well when there is a relationship and positive regard. Stretching colleagues comes through challenging others.

**How to challenge?**

- Ask questions! This is fundamental to coaching and creating a team of independent thinkers (see Chapter 10).
- Training others can be part of the stretch process. However, to encourage others to be inspired, the training needs to be inspiring. It needs to cover ethos, pathos and logos (see Chapter 9).
- Increase the knowledge and skills of the team in their specialist knowledge area (see Chapter 8).

*I'm developing my ability to question, challenge other professionals. That's been quite difficult.*

– SENCO I21

### 4. Motivating self and others

'The in-tray for SEND is never empty'.

**What is this?** Motivation is what gets you out of bed each morning or prompts you to do a task. Each one of us is motivated by different things. For example, intrinsic motivation is what I thrive on. The thrill and joy of completing a task. Yes, I am one of these tick activity lists people. Rewards or accolades do nothing for me. Others, however, need external encouragement of sorts. There is no right or wrong. It's all about knowing what will help me, and others get through both the easy routine tasks and the more infrequent challenging ones.

Top tips:

Since SEND can be a never-ending in-tray, I make sure there are at least a few completion-type tasks in my daily routine.

# DIMENSION 4: INTERPERSONAL SKILLS

**Why does it matter?** Without motivation, apathy and boredom can set in and we are back to the story of *Everybody, Somebody, Anybody, and Nobody* (see Chapter 9).

One of the challenges of the SENCO role is the individual is required to work independently, sometimes on their own and at other times with others. The transition between these two states of 'on their own' and 'with others' can often happen within one hour. There is no transition marker between the two, and dependent on the expected flow of adaption, can cause different internal dynamics.

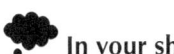 **In your shoes:**

For example:

- **Working on own → working with others**

    'If only I had more time to finish what I was doing. Sometimes these conversations with others go round in circles and it wastes my time. It would be quicker if I did it on my own'.

- **Working on own → working with others**

    'I really enjoyed working with others just now, so many great ideas and we got lots done. I'm now back to finishing this task on my own. It feels empty. I think if someone else was helping, we would probably get this done quicker and move on to the next task'.

 **Question:**

Can you see the paradox?

Most SENCOs will tell you their role is a constant flitting between these two states, and this can also change rapidly, from initially working with SLT, to teachers, parents, a call to the local authority etc.

 **Action task:**

It would be useful to record how much time per week the SENCO works on their own and how often with others. Also, whether the 'others' are internal or external. Many SENCOs seek community with other SENCOs, this is to be expected. However, does this leave them exhausted in terms of then connecting with internal staff, which, in turn, hinders team growth? Again, there are no easy answers.

This quote by a SENCO in relation to how much training they had received intrigued me.

*Nothing [training] since joining my present school, but I am [a] national-level trainer.*
– SENCO Q 81

 **Question:**

How does being a national-level trainer motivate this SENCO and others? Does it increase internal influence? Or can it leave the SENCO feeling more frustrated because externally they are connecting with like-minded people but nothing is happening regularly in-house?

**Self-audit grid for discussions with line managers**

Table 11.1 presents each of the four subdimensions of interpersonal skills. In Chapter 14, I provide a case study example of how this could be used with the other six dimensions of SLIM (Devi, 2022).

Read through the descriptors along the rows and *choose the best fit for this moment in time*. There is no right or wrong answer. It is about knowing where the SENCO currently is and what the potential for growth is.

Once the SENCO has completed this, I would suggest talking through the self-audit with their line manager. In particular, asking if they agree and jointly considering what evidence would support the best-fit judgement.

The discussion should raise further discussion points, such as what are the opportunities for growth around building relationships in-house and externally?

*Table 11.1* Five level descriptors for segments of the interpersonal skills dimension (Devi, 2022)

|  | 1<br>Aware | 2<br>Learning | 3<br>Know | 4<br>Apply | 5<br>Confident |
|---|---|---|---|---|---|
| Active listening | I listen to reactively respond. Whilst people are talking, I am focused on what I will say back to them. I am not sure I always fully hear what they are saying. | I am learning to still my mind and not think I have to have an answer to every problem. I make time to listen and reflect. | I know how to actively listen for both agreement and areas where ideas may differ. I know how to reason this through asking questions if I need more information. | I am applying and demonstrating my listening skills across the full SEND7 so as to build stronger relationships and a deeper understanding of inclusion. | I am confident in listening without the filters of right or wrong to simply hear a wide range of ideas to make informed collaborative decisions. |
| Supporting teams | I support my immediate team of support staff plus teachers when asked. | I am learning to support a wider range of diverse teams to grow in their strengths and address some of their areas of development. | I know how to use different strategies when working with individuals as well as different teams. | I am effectively applying different team management strategies to different situations. I make time to reflect on situations drawing out key learning points that I share with the team. | I am confident in growing, pruning and redefining teams, using agile approaches in different contexts to make all team players feel they have a contribution to make. |

*(Continued)*

Table 11.1 (Continued)

| | 1 Aware | 2 Learning | 3 Know | 4 Apply | 5 Confident |
|---|---|---|---|---|---|
| Stretching colleagues | I challenge colleagues, when necessary, but on the whole, I am uncomfortable with this. | I am learning different ways to challenge colleagues by asking tactful questions and reflecting on any problems they raise to facilitate joint problem-solving. | I know how to effectively challenge different team members so as to stretch them in their implementation of inclusive practice in education. | I am applying a wide range of strategies (including advising, facilitating, mentoring, leading, training and coaching) to support colleagues and others in SEND7. | I am confident in discerning a range of strategies for growth with diverse people and in different contexts. |
| Motivating self and others | I sometimes motivate myself and others to be better at what we do. | I am learning to be intentional about motivating myself and others, using different approaches and reflecting on what is working, when and why. I also see problems as an opportunity for growth. | I know how to ask people about what motivates them and then use this effectively to build greater team input and mutual rapport. | I am applying timely strategies throughout the year to ensure all staff and the SEND7 teams stay on track and remain motivated. | I am confident in motivating myself 95% of the time and others 90% of the time. In situations where my motivation strategy does not work, I reflect, refine and try again. |

SLIM (Devi, 2022): People skills: *Connected leadership (building relationships)*

DIMENSION 4: INTERPERSONAL SKILLS

 **Further reading:**

Devi, A., & Bowers, J. (2022). *Journeying to the Heart of SENCO Wellbeing*. London: Routledge.

 **Question:**

What are your top three takeaways from this chapter?

## Summary

This chapter covered the conversations SENCOs have with themselves and others. It drew on team building and the follow-up of stretch and challenge. More fundamentally though, it considered motivation of self and others. This is relevant for retention.

Chapter 12 looks at dimension 5 and strategic decision-making skills. This is a dual-faceted skill – being strategic and making decisions.

PART 2

# 12 | Dimension 5: Strategic decision-making skills

*Whilst handling day-to-day duties, a SENCO is required to shift school culture, often within the wider context of a multi-academy trust. Therefore, understanding the difference between strategy and long-term planning becomes vital. Hopefully, by now, you are seeing connections between the six dimensions and the wider conceptual framework questions discussed in Part 1.*

*In this chapter, I will unpack the strategic decision-making skills dimension. This consists of four subdimensions: defining a vision, articulating and living out core values, evaluating options and solutions and setting relationship boundaries. Are you surprised by any of these subareas? Most people consider vision, values and solutions (planning) but often omit relationship boundaries.*

### Additional materials:

- Do look at the additional material relating to Chapter 5.

### 1. Defining a vision

*If I see, I believe it and I can achieve it!*

**What is this?** It's the skill of painting a picture that makes it clear to everyone what SEND provision will look like in three years.

**Why does it matter?** Without the picture, the vision becomes open to interpretation, with everyone pushing and pulling in different directions until there is mission drift.

*The only thing worse than being blind is having sight but no vision*

– Helen Keller

Writing a leadership vision isn't easy. The vision serves as a guide to decision-making and staying focused on long-term goals, so it needs to be clear.

For clarity, a mission statement is your 'why'. In England, this has been framed in the Education Inspection Framework (Ofsted, 2019) as intent. A vision statement is, if we were to fulfil our intent, what would that look like?

In an ideal scenario, if we could time travel forward three years, take a photo or video of what we would see and then travel back to show everyone that would make it easier. The potential of what is possible is seen, and whilst many may not believe it (fully) because they have seen it, they can work towards it. So, for example, a new way of working needs to be implemented. When introduced, staff can see that it is a jigsaw piece for the vision, and they are more likely to accept it. A vision holds together the smaller pieces seen along the journey. Sadly, we do not have access to a time machine. Instead, let's walk through a process:

**SENCO:** My vision is for every child in our school to have the support and provision they need.

- Does this actually tell you anything?
- Can you see it?
- Could you recognise it if you arrived?

The majority would possibly answer no to all these questions.

When a SENCO says to me 'My vision is for every child in our school to have the support and provision they need', my response is often, 'What would that look like?' The SENCO then goes on to describe systems, doings, sayings and relatings (Kemmis et al., 2013), which each one of us interprets differently. So, most of us still can't see it.

Yet another SENCO states, 'My vision for SEND in the school is for it to be like an IKEA showroom'. Immediately, everyone sees:

- A streamlined system of walking through the process.
- Cost-effective, but functional with a variety of options.
- DIY flatpacks that need to be constructed, so it's about building around the child.
- An innovative, creative and personalised approach. Not one size fits all.

I led a SENCO workshop once on writing vision. For one of the SENCOs, healthy schools dominated their ethos/agenda. As a result, the vision the SENCO constructed was a pie chart on a plate. Where there would ordinarily be carbohydrates, protein, sweets/sugar, dairy and fruit and vegetables, the SENCO defined what would be seen in the school. This model helped show the proportions of different aspects, so there was prioritisation of effort and resources, but it also pulled it together into a united whole.

TeamADL is an educational service provider that I founded. When we wrote our vision, we started by stating:

- The who – Who is impacted by our vision?
- The impact – What would we see?
- The space – Which dimensions would be affected?

In the end, our vision became, 'Everyone thriving in education, employment and life'. This dovetailed into our existing mission (our purpose) and our core values (mode of operating).

You know you have your vision when you (and others) can see it in part and simultaneously say not there yet! I've also found a vision works when people either say 'That's me' or 'I want in'. That's when you know they have personalised it for themselves. With the 'My vision is for every child in our school to have the support and provision they need' there was no ownership. The IKEA example worked because everyone understood the encounter and it was a Marmite thing – staff either liked IKEA or they didn't, but they knew what it meant.

Action task:

Writing a vision takes time, so this might be a helpful activity to structure your thinking.

Gather several random objects from school and home. Using the format suggested in Table 12.1, list these and next to each share different features of the object. In the third column, write some notes on how you might relate this to SEND. This activity may help you articulate where you are now and where you want to be, i.e. what would be different.

*A few example visions from other industries*

- **Google:** 'To provide access to the world's information in one click'
- **IKEA:** 'To create a better everyday life for the many people'
- **Instagram:** 'Capture and share the world's moments'
- **LinkedIn:** 'Create economic opportunity for every member of the global workforce'
- **TED:** 'Spread ideas'
- **Tesla:** 'To accelerate the world's transition to sustainable energy'

*Table 12.1* Using everyday objects to research possible descriptors for a vision

| Object | Key observable features or functions | How does this relate to SEND? |
| --- | --- | --- |

DIMENSION 5: STRATEGIC DECISION-MAKING

Top tips:

1. Team up with people to help you write a vision. You will gain additional insights into both perspective and use of language.
2. Project your goals for the future – what will look different?
3. Be specific to your setting. Generic visions rarely inspire and, in theory, could be applied to any organisation.
4. Keep it short and simple (KISS). That way, people will remember.

> *I always consider and I always reflect on the different leaders I've had. Whether they've been visionary or mentoring or you know. So, I think I take the elements, I think worked, that I worked well under and try to implement all those things into how I lead.*
> – SENCO I16

## 2. Articulating and living out core values

*Who I am speaks louder than what I do.*

**What is this?** Core values are more than principles. Principles articulate the way you do things, but core values reflect your beliefs. In turn, these beliefs shape thoughts, behaviours, speech and focus.

**Why it matters?** In Chapter 5, I mentioned autopilot. Values keep you on track. They connect your inner world (beliefs) with the outer world (actions). This connection is often called authenticity or integrity and speaks to your character. Character is vital for any leader, and we notice it when it is favourable or noble, but also when it is missing and hypocrisy is evident. Character is a neutral word and how you as a leader define and imbibe it could make or break your legacy.

In your shoes:

Write five core beliefs you have about inclusion or SEND. Pay close attention to the language you use. Revisit this after a week; did you see these beliefs in your actions and decisions?

Action task:

Research a list of values and pick out seven that resonate with your beliefs. Check these seven words using a dictionary and thesaurus. Are there any better words? Narrow your seven values down to three or four. Ask yourself, how do they connect and what would others see in my behaviour?

Case study:

As a SENCO, Jenita was always telling her teaching staff that SEND is everyone's responsibility and it isn't difficult. Her key phrase was, 'Together, we can do this!' Jenita's own behaviour showed she was always working late and on weekends, always stressed and always running around complaining about something. The staff didn't believe Jenita when she tried to persuade them that SEND wasn't difficult. They saw her working and didn't want that in their lives. So, in the end, they didn't do anything.

Questions:

- What mixed messages was Jenita giving out through her own behaviour?
- Why did the lack of coherence between what she said and what she did become a problem for the staff?

In your shoes:

Ask some of your trusted colleagues whether you are giving out any mixed messages.

> *To be honest with you I think that the strategic thinking, the blue-sky thinking are sometimes the first things to go because inevitably if you've got some issues with some students and you're called to deal with that there's always been some firefighting throughout the day, and you always get some parents that show up unannounced and demand to be seen.*
>
> – SENCO I19

### 3. Evaluating options and solutions

*Do you focus on the problem or possible opportunities?*

**What is this?** This is about approaching every situation as if it were for the first time. Einstein is attributed for saying, 'If you do what you've always done, you will get what you've always got'. As a scientist, he knew the importance of repeated trials with changed variables. SENCOs need to see every new situation afresh with a new set of eyes, building on the experience of the past, not just repeating it.

**Why does it matter?** Repetition of the same response only works if all other conditions are stable; we know this is not the case. Talking to SENCOs at different stages of their life, I get the impression many believe there is a standard way to respond to all situations.

# DIMENSION 5: STRATEGIC DECISION-MAKING

This is often advocated through books, speakers and social media. In fact, even the SEND CoP 2015 implies a set of standard procedures. However, what is missing is the dynamic environment (see Figures 1.1 and 8.3). If SENCOs respond 'the same way' to each scenario, three subsequent problems are likely to follow.

1) **Cumulative errors become the norm**. Imagine you measure and cut a length of ribbon. You then use that cut piece to measure subsequent pieces. Over time you will see the length of the cut pieces change because exact measurements are not being used. Similar scenarios happen in the SEND arena; SENCOs adopt the measured response to a different problem to solve their specific problem. I have seen this at the identification level and whole school development.

2) **Key information is missed**. Adopting the 'same as previous' mentality, professional curiosity fails to ask further questions that may be pertinent to the new scenario. Again, I have seen this at the identification level and whole school development. I was training EHCP panel members in a local authority and we were diligently working through a case. In the live case used, all the paperwork kept reiterating, 'It is reported Joanna has X condition' (a medical condition). On the basis of this statement, the panel decided to award an EHCP. As the facilitator of the training, I then asked, 'Where is the evidence of a formal diagnosis of X?' The panel checked again and there had been no formal diagnosis. They based their assumption on a proposed hypothesis that had been repeated several times in the paperwork but had no evidence of proof. It may have been that Joanna had X, but no one (at any level) had investigated and knew for sure.

## Question:

How many EHCPs have been constructed on the basis of a hypothesis as opposed to an evidence-based diagnosis?

*[Additional note: In my personal opinion, both the EHCA and EHCP panels are flawed in the way they operate. The training above was designed to create an evidence trail of consistent and equitable decisions. I have also long argued that a standard template for the process would make the fairness of decisions more transparent. Both these aspects remain a work in progress for England. We currently have a system where the paperwork is personalised, but the process isn't. The SEND Reforms (2010–2018) set out to create personalised processes with standardised systems. That, in my opinion, is why the system is failing. We have implemented the exact opposite of what we set out to do.]*

3) **Professional boredom and complacency can set in**. Routine is healthy; however, professional performance is possibly optimised when there are routines that allow a degree of creativity and innovation. This is agency in practice (see Chapter 6). Patterns of behaviour are the manifestation of thought. This self-talk and mental imagery are often referred to as 'thought self-leadership' (TSL) (Neck & Manz, 1992; Quinteiro et al., 2016). Constructive TSL (which is voluntary and self-directed) can

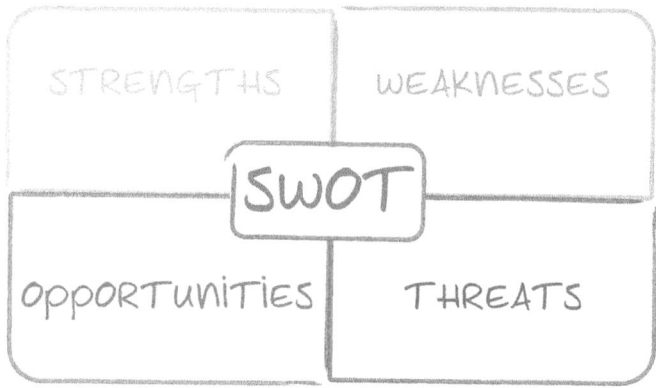

*Figure 12.1* Four aspects of the SWOT analysis model

result in work fulfilment (Neck & Milliman, 1994). Moreover, Lai and Kapstad (2009) propose that there exists a curvilinear relationship between self-efficacy and perceived competence mobilisation. As such, the adverse can also be true; negative self-talk and lack of self-efficacy can result in job dissatisfaction. Throughout the study, SENCOs expressed different views about themselves and their roles.

Action task:

One way to address this is to have a responsive framework to analyse each problem. This can also help to separate the facts from opinions, thereby enhancing the SENCO's ability to evaluate options and solutions for each new case.

Some organisations/sectors use SWOT analysis as a framework to consider different dimensions of a problem (Figure 12.1).

Generally speaking, most situations can be translated onto a 2 x 2 matrix. The challenge for skilled leaders is to figure out the dimensions of the matrix. A useful 2 x 2 matrix for SENCO time management is the Eisenhower Matrix. Take some time to research this. It could change your working patterns and way of thinking.

### 4. Setting relationship boundaries

*There is more to me than just work!*

**What is this?** A set of boundaries with the SEND7. These boundaries can be around time, communications and expectations.

## DIMENSION 5: STRATEGIC DECISION-MAKING

**Why does it matter?** Essentially, many SENCOs see the role as pastoral rather than leading. Part of this perception relates to the motivation for applying, which I have already addressed. However, a bigger element is the possibility that they make the most difference and get the greatest feedback (good and bad). So, it becomes a priority. Good relationships are essential for any career. However, there needs to be boundaries to protect individuals and ensure people aren't taken for granted or advantage of.

Part of communicating boundaries is about learning to say, 'No' (politely, of course). Is there likely to be a comeback? For sure. But saying yes (to keep the peace) sets a precedent for further actions and interactions. It can also create passive-aggressive behaviours in the system. I find distinguishing between peacekeepers and peacemakers a way to avoid the SENCO becoming a people pleaser (Devi & Bowers, 2022).

**Peacekeepers:** These are individuals who will do anything to avoid conflict, even if it means compromising their own core values. It's the 'as long as everyone is happy, all will be well' mentality. In the short term or as a single episode, it might work. But it doesn't work long term and rarely is everyone happy!

**Peacemakers:** This is an intentional process of listening to everyone, but then skilfully managing conflict to find an agreed solution through the stated values and vision. In this scenario, some people will be upset or have to compromise, but in the long term, it is a better outcome.

There is a fine line between peacekeeping and peacemaking, and this comes with intentional practice and reflection for growth.

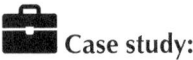
**Case study:**

As a teaching SENCO, who also had Senior Leader responsibilities, managing my time was critical. We wanted to have an open-door policy for parents, and I also wanted to stop staff corridor conversations. Sometimes I would be headed to my class to teach and a member of staff would stop me to talk about SEND. My head space was in the curriculum, not SEND. As a result, I set up SEND Surgeries. Every Wednesday from 3:30 pm to 4:30 pm, I would be in my classroom. The dates were advertised at the start of term and regularly throughout.

**Week 1:** Any parent/carer could drop by to talk about any concerns they had.

**Week 2:** Any staff member could stop by to raise concerns about a child in their class or provision.

This stopped all the corridor conversations, staff became much better at problem-solving themselves and parents knew they could approach me and I would take note.

The structure enabled me to follow up conversations with speed. For example, a parent raises a concern in week one, I ask the teacher to come and see me in week two and vice versa.

As my role evolved to the local authority level, I emulated the same process across a local authority area. I would encourage MAT SEND leads to consider how they structure their time and availability across schools and for SENCOs.

**Self-audit grid for discussions with line managers**

Table 12.2 presents each of the four dimensions of strategic decision-making skills, building in capacity for growth if circumstances change, year on year. In Chapter 14, I provide a case study example of how this could be used with the other six dimensions of SLIM (Devi, 2022).

Read through the descriptors along the rows and *choose the best fit for this moment in time*. There is no right or wrong answer. It is about knowing where the SENCO currently is and what the potential for growth is.

Once the SENCO has completed this, I would suggest talking through the self-audit with their line manager. In particular, asking if they agree and jointly considering what evidence would support the best-fit judgement.

The discussion should raise further discussion points, such as what are the opportunities for deepening understanding.

## DIMENSION 5: STRATEGIC DECISION-MAKING

Table 12.2 Five level descriptors for segments of the strategic decision-making skills dimension (Devi, 2022)

| | 1<br>Aware | 2<br>Learning | 3<br>Know | 4<br>Apply | 5<br>Confident |
|---|---|---|---|---|---|
| Defining a vision | I have an idea of where I would like SEND provision to be in three years' time, but I cannot articulate it to anyone else. Sometimes, this is because I think I know what my vision is, but I cannot see it. | I am learning to use metaphors and concrete objects to articulate my vision, so others can see it and there is little room for ambiguity. I am learning to pay close attention to my choice of words. | I know exactly how to articulate my vision of SEND provision to others, whilst remaining open to feedback for growth. | I am applying various tools of persuasion for the SEND7 to not only 'know' my vision for SEND provision, but for them to recognise the part they can play in making it happen. | I am confident in my vision and how I have articulated it to others (including the frequency of communication) and I am confident together we will achieve it. |
| Articulating and living our core values | I have an idea of my values and how this links to my understanding of inclusion. | I am learning to narrow my core values down to five key concepts and link this to national policy plus the broader vision of our school, set by SLT. | I know how to refine my values further to three core beliefs and reflect on how they relate to both everyday practice and the wider strategic aims of developing our inclusive practice. | I am intentionally applying my three core values to day-to-day decisions. Others can see this reflected in my words and actions. Team members recognise my core values as the premise for decision-making. | I am confident in my three core values; communicating them well and using them effectively to lead others into applying them too. |

*(Continued)*

Table 12.2 (Continued)

| | 1<br>Aware | 2<br>Learning | 3<br>Know | 4<br>Apply | 5<br>Confident |
|---|---|---|---|---|---|
| Evaluating options and solutions | I tend to think in black-or-white scenarios. I can see a faint light at the end of the tunnel. | I am learning to intentionally look at all options, consider a wide variety of solutions and then make an informed choice. | I know a core group of people in my network that I can approach face-to-face to discuss a wide range of solutions to any problems we are currently experiencing. | I am applying a structured approach and methodology to reviewing and researching different options and solutions to situations. Others are able to see my consistent methods and emulate them. | I am confident in dealing with complex situations, where the way forward could yield different circumstances depending on which option is chosen. Risk is both calculated and assessed at all stages. |
| Setting relationship boundaries | I just like to ensure everyone gets on. I believe part of my role is making others happy. | I am learning to set boundaries in my professional relationships. I am learning to balance my head and heart when I act with my hands. | I know how and when to pick my battles. I am neither a 'bull in a China shop' nor someone who avoids conversations I perceive to be difficult. I am evenly tempered, even when I have to ask questions to challenge issues. | I am applying emotional intelligence to all my conversations with others, showing heightened awareness of their needs, but also boldly stating my views for consideration. | I am confident in relationship building and knowing when and how to put healthy boundaries in place. I am building rapport, but also handling difficult conversations when they arise without fear or prejudice. |

SLIM (Devi, 2022): Strategic decision-making skills: *Connected leadership (shared vision and purpose)*

 **Question:**

What are your top three takeaways from this chapter?

## Summary

This chapter covered strategic decision-making skills. Whilst most people consider vision, values and planning, this chapter additionally suggested relationship boundaries as an important subdimension for strategies to be effective.

Chapter 13 focuses on dimension 6, the final dimension of SLIM (Devi, 2022), namely, professional skills. It raises different dimensions of a SENCO's emotional capital.

PART 2

# 13 | Dimension 6: Professional skills

The sixth dimension enables SENCOs to self-manage in challenging circumstances. Working with multiple stakeholders (SEND7 and SEND8 for some), the SENCO has to embed core professional skills to maintain their wellbeing, as well as continue to move things forward, sometimes uphill. Naturally, there is an overlap and interconnectedness amongst these six dimensions, but the crucial question is, 'What next?' This leads to dimension 7 and determining further growth through CPD.

> *I don't think I am incredibly effective. I'm like a headless chicken doing lots of things I need to be rationalised.* **An effective SENCO would have an effective agenda of where the school was going. A clear understanding of obviously the practice. And then that strategic plan and overview really of what everybody is doing at every level and how that's all linked together so, it's a beautiful and seamless transfer and everybody does what they're supposed to.**
>
> – SENCO I11

Working in education is rarely as simple and connected as SENCO I11 implies! It takes intentionality, and so this dimension unpacks four professional skills that emerged from the research (Devi, 2022).

Emotional capital is a part of connected leadership.

**Reminder** (from Part 2 introduction):

- **Transformational leadership** translates to the four factors of idealised influence, inspirational motivation, intellectual stimulation and individualised consideration (Northouse, 2019).
- **Connected leadership** embraces emotional capital, shared vision and purpose, and a focus on building relationships, not just maintaining them (Tian et al., 2016).

'Capital' is a term used to imply an asset. As practitioners, you are endowed with non-financial assets that aid your success. This was very much the thinking behind the conceptual framework (see Chapter 6).

DIMENSION 6: PROFESSIONAL SKILLS

See Figure 13.1 as an example.

- Social capital pertains to the benefits of having relationships with people and groups, including families, clubs, workplaces and other organisations.
- Human capital covers the knowledge, habits, personality traits and creativity that enable people to be economically successful.
- Emotional capital is the ability to use emotions effectively for many purposes, embracing self-esteem, self-efficacy and self-regulation.

 **In your shoes:**

Talk about the emotional capital triad with a trusted colleague or your line manager. What's working? What could be better or different?

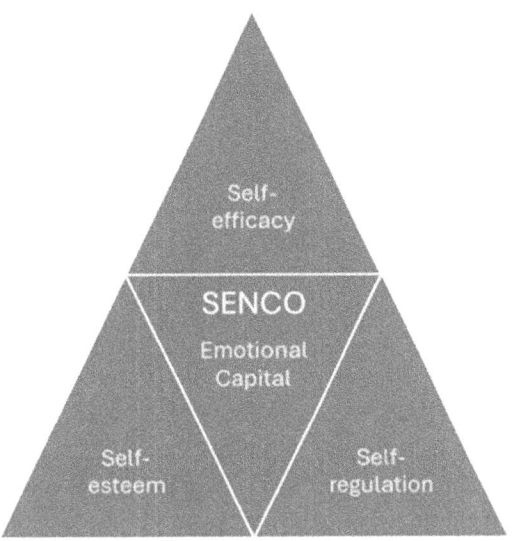

*Figure 13.1* Emotional capital triad of a SENCO

## 1. Self-management

**What is this?** Self-management is about being organised, understanding the diverse dimensions of the role and transitioning well between 'working on your own' and 'working with others' (see Chapter 11). Self-management requires both agility and continuous reflective approaches that intentionally focus on possibilities rather than problems and difficulties. As stated in Chapter 2, being a SENCO isn't for everyone!

**Why does it matter?** There is no standard day for a SENCO, what is required changes within days and between days. In such a dynamic environment, having a stable self-management system helps to realign leadership and management skills in quiet times and during storms!

Many SENCOS will say, like SENCO I8, 'I'm organised'. However, being organised in a stable world with a structured work routine is very different from 'staying organised' in a dynamic environment. The result is that many SENCOs end up doing more, as opposed to doing less and doing differently. This has a knock-on effect on workload and wellbeing.

## 2. Time management

*[I'm] tired of the paperwork ... I want to work with the children more. I'm good at what I do when I have the time.*

– SENCO I25

*I regularly go into the classrooms to support within the classroom so I'm very much a hands-on SENCO. I'm not just stuck in the office doing paperwork all the time.*

– SENCO I26

*Submitting paperwork – that is a huge part of my role.*

– SENCO I15

**What is this?** Within the SENCO world, time management is about creating structure in an unstructured environment. As well as relationship boundaries, this involves boundaries around expectations and defining realistic time allocations for different tasks and activities. It involves prioritisation.

**Why does it matter?** SENCOs without a structured time management system often experience regular episodic burnout or stress. Over time, this can manifest into long-term stress, and many SENCOs adopt the false belief that this is the norm. No job should involve continued heightened levels of stress.

One of the questions I often ask SENCOs is, 'Do you work from rest (i.e. refreshed) or to rest (i.e. exhaustion)?' The majority reply, the latter, yet they know working 'from rest' is much more productive.

**What is rest?** It is the recognition that we are not superhuman, superheroes or perfect. Therefore, demarcation points are needed to define the end of the day to switch off, and also the end of the week (i.e. weekend) for renewal and celebration, plus a focus on other matters of importance other than work. Work is part of what we do, but it isn't the sole purpose as to why we exist. Productivity is important within the seasonal cycles of the day, the week, the month and the term. When SENCOs push through to work when they are tired, the propensity to make mistakes and for the tasks to take longer is much higher.

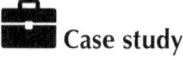Case study:

As a SENCO, class teacher and senior leader, I had wide-ranging responsibilities. BUT I never worked after 5:30 pm (weekdays) or on weekends. I knew I was more productive in the mornings (optimal times for working), and I valued family time. During the holidays, I would rest first and then prepare for the new term or year. By establishing daily, weekly and seasonal cessation activities, I found that I was more focused and productive during the timeframe allocated.

**Further reading:**

Devi, A. (2016). *Take time – time management strategies and case studies for SENCOs* [eBook]. London: Optimus Publishing.

## 3. Endurance

*I am conscientious.*

– SENCO I3

*I am committed.*

– SENCO I1

**What is this?** SENCOs cannot be sprinters or even relay team members. They are marathon runners. Some SENCOs want to achieve everything like a sprinter, but soon recognise they are expending their energy in the wrong type of event and in the wrong way. Sprinters and marathon runners train differently and require different levels of stamina. Their lifestyles are also quite different.

**Why does it matter?** Without investing in the endurance muscle, SENCOs may try to acquire results too quickly and in doing so risk losing the support of their team. There is an African proverb,

*If you want to go fast, go alone. If you want to go further, go together.*

Marquet (2015), when talking about turning the ship around, highlights the importance of consistent one-degree moves. Co-ordinating the SEND7/SEND8, SENCOs lead the largest team in schools; therefore, consistent one-degree moves often result in a significant shift by the end of the year (see Chapter 11).

Endurance and perseverance are often used interchangeably. However, endurance is about the capacity to withstand hardship or adversity, and perseverance is about determination to succeed towards the goal.

*I am hopeful that these challenges can be overcome.*

– SENCO I9

Throughout the research, endurance was seen repeatedly (by SENCOs) as an attribute used to be in the role and access CPD, to drive change and pursue personal goals. However, without perseverance, long-term sustainability may be compromised.

## 4. Persuasiveness

**What is this?** Communication, listening and people skills have already been addressed in previous chapters. In this context, though, persuasiveness is linked to endurance for self and others.

It's all about self-talk and encouraging others.

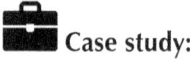 **Case study:**

When I've taken part in physical challenges in the past, I often feel like giving up. It gets too hard, I'm tired, hungry, cold or it's raining. But equally, I have a voice that tells me, if you keep going, think of the celebration on completion – think about how many others will benefit from the sponsorship you have collected. And so, I choose to keep going because that voice is stronger and has persuaded me, over the other voice, to keep going.

This is true for the SENCO too.

Annually, I support our local marathon team by volunteering to be a marshal along the route. It never ceases to amaze me how much a little encouragement by spectators/volunteers or distributing jelly babies really motivates the runners, especially those struggling with the heat or muscle pain.

This is true for the teams SENCOs lead.

**Why does it matter?** There are lots of voices, and it isn't always about the loudest. But which voice will help sustain leaders and followers to keep going? That's the most persuasive.

We know the SEND7/SEND8 bring different voices, expectations and perspectives to the table, and this is to be encouraged. Part of the SENCO role is navigating these differences to a common solution, where inevitably there will be compromises. Creating a shared atmosphere of acceptance and sustained commitment is where the SENCO will need to harness their skills of persuasion the most.

### Self-audit grid for discussions with line managers

Table 13.1 presents each of the four dimensions of professional skills SENCOs need to intentionally invest time in developing and reviewing. In Chapter 14, I provide a case study example of how this could be used with the other six dimensions of SLIM (Devi, 2022).

Table 13.1 Five level descriptors for segments of the professional skills dimension (Devi, 2022)

| | 1 Aware | 2 Learning | 3 Know | 4 Apply | 5 Confident |
|---|---|---|---|---|---|
| Self-management | I get by doing what I can and when I can. Some days I am effective, but most days not. | I am learning to develop more self-awareness about when I am most effective, what I need and how I work best with others. | I know my strengths and areas for development. I am not following the crowd, but seeking out a deeper understanding of who I am as a SENCO based on the journey I have had and the skills I bring to the role. | I am applying a wide range of skills to improve my proficiency as a SENCO. I recognise it is a balance between leadership and management and that I do not have to know all the answers, all the time. | I am a confident leader, reflective and reflexive. I invest in time with/for others, but I also carve out time for myself. |
| Time management | I do not have a real structure for managing my time. I just do what comes up or is a priority. | I am learning to set a structure for my SENCO working time. This enables me to put in place boundaries and focus on activities, not just a long list of tasks. | I know my most productive working times, so I structure the most difficult tasks during this optimal productivity zone. I know how to streamline and delegate. I plan ahead. | I am applying different approaches to my time management by regularly reviewing both my methods and changing circumstances I recognise working in the SEND arena and there are many aspects that are constantly open to change. This is helping to develop my agility as a leader. | I confidently accept my inbox will never be empty. I actively seek help when I need it and I share with those who line manage me different strategies I am employing to manage my time and wellbeing. I model good working practices for the team. |

(Continued)

## 7 DIMENSIONS OF HIGHLY EFFECTIVE SENCOS

Table 13.14 (Countinued)

| | 1 Aware | 2 Learning | 3 Know | 4 Apply | 5 Confident |
|---|---|---|---|---|---|
| Endurance | I quickly get despondent when things do not work out. I want to keep going, but I do not know how. | I am learning different ways to increase my endurance during difficult situations. I recognise I do not have to carry this burden by myself and talking things through face-to-face with a trusted other is an option. | I know my limitations, but equally, I value opportunities for stretch. I know I need to talk to my line manager when things get too much, and every situation is an opportunity for learning and growth. | I can apply different reflective methodologies to help me process daily, weekly and termly workloads. I am intentional about not carrying any baggage from one season to the next, as this hinders my productivity. | I am confident in not always getting things right or always needing to show I am coping. I can learn from tricky situations, and I have a strong network around me that can come alongside me and coach me to think of new ways of working. |
| Persuasiveness | I just tell people what I want them to do and I expect them to do it. | I am learning to understand different persuasion strategies people need to mobilise them into action. I enjoy experimenting with these to see what works best, when and with whom. | I know at least three different approaches I can take when trying to persuade the SEND7 to take on their level of responsibility in supporting SEND learners. | I am able to apply transition strategies between different modes of persuasion to match the audience I am interacting with. | I am confident in navigating a way forward for SEND and enabling others to take part. I am confident in knowing sometimes I will get it wrong, but through feedback, I can learn better ways of working. |

SLIM (Devi, 2022): Professional skills: Connected leadership (*emotional capital*)

Read through the descriptors along the rows and *choose the best fit for this moment in time*. There is no right or wrong answer. It is about knowing where the SENCO currently is and what the potential for growth is.

Once the SENCO has completed this, I would suggest talking through the self-audit with their line manager. In particular, asking if they agree and jointly considering what evidence would support the best-fit judgement.

The discussion should raise further discussion points, such as what are the opportunities for continuous professional development.

Action task:

Before we look at the seventh dimension, reflect on this social media question:

> Hi. I'm looking for some CPD options as I haven't had anything specific to the role in over four years. I have the NASENCO award and an MA in education. What else can we access to further our development? I work in a small primary school currently so don't think the specialist knowledge route is necessarily going to be the best, but it does interest me. Thanks.

Questions:

- What are your observations?
- What would you advise this SENCO?
- What questions about the SENCO career trajectory arise for you?

## Summary

This chapter covered dimension 6 of SLIM (Devi, 2022) – professional skills. Due consideration was given to the social, human and emotional capital of the role, homing in on self-management, time management, endurance and persuasiveness. In concluding the final dimension of SLIM, the groundwork has been laid to consider the practical workings of a SEND Leader Integrated Model, which will be demonstrated in Chapter 14.

# 14 | Dimension 7: Structured approach to SENCO Continuous Professional Development (CPD)

PART 2

*In the preceding chapters, I presented a case for a different model of SENCO development and practical ways in which this can be enacted through the SEND Leader Integrated Framework (SLIM) (Devi, 2022). In this chapter, I bring all six elements of SLIM together to consider 27 potential models of continuous professional development (CPD).*

Many researchers (Essex et al., 2019; Mintz, 2019; Robinson, 2017) concur about the need for ongoing professional development for SEND and inclusion. In reference to teachers, Coldwell (2017) further states that professional development is essential for retention. The literature on SENCO professional development has mainly been shared by Klaus Wedell (1999, 2002, 2012, 2016, 2018, 2019, 2020) and Lewis and Ogilvie (2003) looking at the interactions of an online (Parker & Bowell, 1998) communities of practice (Wenger, 1998) forum. Dobson and Douglas (2020b) highlight that many SENCOs are attracted to the role as they see it as an opportunity for professional development.

Professional development (PD) is a collective term for support, activities and programmes that enable teachers to develop as professionals (Coldwell, 2017). These can be formal and informal. Examples of support include coaching and mentoring. One-off training sessions are regarded as activities. Programmes, on the other hand, are structured processes that can include opportunities for action-based research, deeper reflection and lesson study. The key indicator of success is the transference into the classroom and improving educational outcomes for children and young people (Leask & Younie, 2013; Scutt & Harrison, 2019). Research shows professional development can have an impact on teacher effectiveness (Cordingley et al., 2015). *Continuous* professional development shifts PD to become a strategic driver that enhances staff development, recruitment, retention, wellbeing and organisational improvement. Scutt and Harrison (2019) argue that CPD needs to be a continuous learning process to truly measure effectiveness. In other words, PD focuses on the individual, whereas CPD is organisation-wide (Coldwell, 2017). This is relevant since the journey in Figure 3.2 (Chapter 3) highlights a professional's journey from individual teacher with classroom responsibilities to whole-school leadership. Therefore, in this chapter, emphasis has been placed on CPD. Robinson (2017) argues that CPD is regarded as a decisive factor in developing inclusive education for SEN (Forlin, 2010, 2012; Bač áková & Closs, 2013; Makopoulou et al., 2019).

# DIMENSION 7: SENCO CPD

## Protected time to do the job or protected CPD time?

My research challenged the current paradigm that purports SENCOs should 'automatically' be part of the senior leadership team (Chapter 7), as well as current thinking around 'protected time to do the role' (Curran et al., 2018; Curran et al., 2019, 2021; Curran & Boddison, 2021). Instead, I propose a structure for **protected** *continuous professional development* time to ensure SENCOs continue to invest in their identity and agency (Sherman & Teemant, 2021), thereby enhancing their impact and influence.

The model put forward to protect 'doing the job' time (Curran et al., 2018, 2019, 2021; Curran & Boddison, 2021) was based on several variables, including how many children are on the SEND register, to what degree of need and the size of the school. This makes it an unstable and fluctuating model, with the potential for numbers to rise and fall each year. Either way, such a model does not provide SENCOs with job security or scope to grow in the role. In the absence of anything else, many latched onto this model and used the lower-than-average, average and higher-than-average tables to argue for better working conditions. The original study (Curran et al., 2018) involved organisations representing practitioners, researchers and trade unions. The formula used to calculate the guidance for SENCO time allocation was never published in the public domain and, in many respects, this went against the government agenda at the time of 'Levelling Up'. In other words, the national government believes the percentage of children and young people identified with SEND should more or less even out in each setting across the country. Again, whilst this may be a strong mathematical model, the reality is very different. From an SLT perspective, 'protected time to do the job' using a formula has financial implications. Imagine if numbers change significantly mid-year, or as in my experience as a SENCO, numbers on the roll fall and two schools amalgamate. In contrast, annual protected CPD time and opportunities for the SENCO can be budgeted and planned for. It is a stable approach to retention.

In 1988, as part of wider curriculum reforms, the Secretary of State for Education (England) introduced five mandatory days for teacher training. These subsequently became called 'Inset days' (i.e. in-service training days). SENCOs are qualified teachers, and so they have the five dedicated days of training, but no mandatory time every year to upskill themselves as SENCOs. There is also nothing stipulated in legislation, policy or practice to suggest that at least one of their five inset days should be for the SENCO role. This, in many respects, was one of the starting questions for my research.

- Why are SENCOs in England not allocated any statutory training days?
- If annual statutory training days for SENCOs were to be a reality, then how would they decide what training to embark on in terms of content and/or methodology?

The initial SENCO induction qualification is intense and expensive, so many senior leaders subsequently argue, 'No further training is required'. Whilst the outcomes of the SENCO induction qualification are published in the public domain, the actual qualification is surrounded by mystic and commercial sensitivity. Therefore, anyone not involved in this arena would not fully know what the SENCO is qualified to do as a result. The basic premise being simply that the SENCO must pass within three years of appointment. Under the NASENCO, some SLTs used to ask the SENCO to share their research project outcome with staff on completion. However, this was the exception, rather than the norm.

> *They allowed me to do the SENCO as [a] leader qualification which adds credits to us. I never went any further with [it] because time wise it just became difficult.*
> – SENCO I2

Some SENCOs also suggest there was a perverse incentive not to invest in the CPD of a SENCO. Progression could imply stepping up or moving on, thus leaving the school in the dilemma of advertising and appointing for this statutory role. The following **case study** shows the challenges of the identity and skills transition after becoming a SENCO:

> *For many SENCOs it's a one-way road. Once you are a SENCO you are rarely considered for other roles. If it is a school that does not have the SENCO on the SLT then there is rarely an opportunity to progress to this, and SENCOs are not considered for head of department roles such as science or English (which is fair alongside the SENCO role) … but to divert to another path entirely is very difficult. We almost specialise ourselves out of a role. To use a personal example: I am a trained secondary science teacher who has taught it to a group of GCSE students just once in my 25 years of teaching. Why? Because my secondary SENCO role has always seen me allocated the students with weak literacy skills lower down the school in order to boost them before they reach the older phases. I became a specialist in delivering phonics-based programmes (interventions but replaced the student English lessons) to address needs, but in doing so was no longer skilled in teaching GCSE science or even KS3 English. There is a danger that as more schools lose their SENCOs due to the pressures they are under, those SENCOs will find themselves 'specialised out of the market' should they want to return to mainstream teaching. I suspect the problem is less pronounced at primary than it is at secondary.*
> – SENCO Q10

Equally, SENCO I9 highlighted that governor support was critical for success, although the governor's perception of success and effectiveness was considerably different to hers. As a result, governors often blocked requests for CPD.

> *I asked if I could have some professional leadership training because we were going into the trust, so we were all a little bit jittery I suppose about that. I can't think why. And I asked for some training and governors turned that down because they didn't feel like it was money well spent.*

SENCOs who did undertake any form of professional development shared that only occasionally were these decisions made in conjunction with their colleagues and leaders

## DIMENSION 7: SENCO CPD

in school ('so I had asked to go on those courses because I knew that they would be helpful for that child' – SENCO I8). More often was the case that the decisions were made independently ('my CPD is mostly self-directed – SENCO I9), paid for by the SENCOs themselves ('[I] have expertise due to the training I have selected and paid for myself over the years and undertaken in their own time' – SENCO Q84) and in their own time ('self-training in own time' – SENCO Q37). In some cases, the leadership was not aware of the SENCO undertaking any training, due to a lack of structures ('So, I've not yet had performance management and I've been here … three years' – SENCO I11). In effect, there was no wider sharing with colleagues and line managers.

In other words, any ongoing SENCO training:

- **Has to be requested with clear outcomes stated.** This is not unreasonable; however, should this relate to individual children's needs (specialist knowledge) or strategic leadership skills development? Who knows and decides?
- **Is self-directed.** The SENCO basically decides. What would be more effective is a discussion with their line managers and CPD leads.
- **Paid for by the SENCO.** This was repeatedly shared by many SENCOs across the country.
- **In the SENCOs' own time.** Again, another common theme. This possibly creates a disparity amongst SENCOs, as it affects their outside work life.
- **Is pointless as nobody is interested in monitoring SENCO development.** The term 'SENCO' has over time come to mean *everything and yet nothing*.

Where discussions did take place with their line managers, SENCOs identified three criteria that determine CPD decisions:

1) **Need/interest.** Both were seen as motivational factors; however, 'need' often being determined by the school leadership (e.g. 'I had to do the access arrangement training; it was agreed at my interview' or 'it will be good on your CV' – SENCO I2) and interest was driven by the SENCO (e.g. 'it would be things that I wanted to do that I'd look for myself. So, I know that I want to do a course on dyslexia, it would probably just the free, it is free at the moment. But I'll find that, and I'll do that' – SENCO I18)
2) **Availability.** This related to method (online, face-to-face) and time. (e.g. 'I compiled through different groups and forums that I'm on. There were lots of lists of training and CPD out there … then this is what is out there for you' – SENCO I7). Availability doesn't always imply the right opportunity or quality.
3) **Cost.** This often proved a key factor, with many SENCOs accessing 'free' training and one SENCO suggesting that over lockdown, she had been 'CPD-ed out!' Those accessing free training were not able to articulate how they quality assured any input or even used what they had learnt. Equally, those self-funding were led by personal choices rather than strategic impact. So, usefulness related to enjoyment, rather than application.

> *I would like further training for specific learning difficulties, but my trust will not support this due to funding. I would also like nurture training but unfortunately there is no money for this, and I cannot afford to self-fund.*
> – SENCO Q77

The process was seen as a negotiation process, within the context of wider school priorities, although many stipulate how CPD choices are very 'self-directed' (SENCO I6). The triad of need/interest, availability and cost was seen as a coherent approach for agreeing to CPD. None of the SENCOs linked their CPD to the strategic development of the school. The majority linked CPD to their self-satisfaction and determination to progress, although the journey of interviewee 9 over several years reflects how her own perseverance made it part of the school processes,

> *I made the decision a few years ago that if I actually wanted to develop meaningful, high-quality CPD for myself, I would have to initiate that and get on and bloody do it. So, I made that decision …then I thought okay what shall I do? I used my NASENCO to take a year off and do a Master's in Education. Then I went ahead and did some professional leadership training through the Open University… So, I just drove that myself.*
> – SENCO I9

Note here, SENCO I9 left the role to pursue her own CPD. There is possibly more to this narrative, however, it demonstrates why retention is compromised without CPD.

> *You do your own training and research online and know who to contact as experts in the LA.*
> – SENCO Q74

In my research, SENCOs on SLT did not receive any more favourable CPD opportunities than those not on SLT. Therefore, simply positioning a SENCO on the senior leadership team, as others (Szwed, 2007; Pearson, 2008; Oldham & Radford, 2011; Pearson et al., 2015, Done et al., 2016a; Curran, 2019; Plender, 2019, Curran & Boddison, 2021) have argued, would not have the desired impact of increased influence and agency.

Additionally, as part of the SENCO 'authoritative functions' (Regulation 50, SEND Regs, 2014), SENCOs are required to train others. So, the fundamental question being:

> **If SENCOs are not the recipients of any continuous professional development programme, how can they possibly train others?**

I'm sure many would agree the initial induction qualification will only take SENCOs so far in fulfilling their role. More ongoing input is required.

## Three areas for consideration when accessing CPD

### *Time allocation*

One of the biggest barriers to accessing CPD is time. The following case study of a SENCO highlights the progression to SLT at a cost to the SENCO role and the strategic element of promoting inclusion. Therefore, whilst whole-school influence and responsibility have increased (to position this SENCO on SLT), it has not helped to further inclusion. Thus, creating a tension between different elements of Regulation 50.

> *Personally, I have been fortunate as I have received ample training in both schools I have/am doing the role. The role has definitely become more strategic. In my previous school I was not on the senior leadership team – however I began to look for a new role in the summer term of 2019 and more roles are now on advertised the leadership team. This has its obvious benefits, but now as Assistant Headteacher a lot of my time is taken up with the day-to-day running of the school and this gives me less time to concentrate on inclusion.*
> – SENCO Q51

**Additional materials:**

- Suggested annual calendar based on the legislative definition of the SENCO role (see Chapter 2).

In this research, the majority of SENCOs had additional roles that related to other vulnerable group pupils, for example, looked after children and those for whom English is an additional language. Others led on safeguarding, mental health and equality, which are substantial roles in themselves and could pose a time/priority conflict for SENCOs. Even with these additional roles, the majority were not on the SLT. At the other end of the additional role spectrum, one was a first aider and lunchtime supervisor. Curran et al. (2021) suggest these additional roles may distract and divert time allocated to the SENCO role. Equally, the passage of time can affect knowledge and understanding, as illustrated by this quote from SENCO I12:

> *To be honest I did my SENCO so long ago in 2013 I don't know whether it is the same anymore. And if I'm honest I can't remember what I did. It seems all [a] bit of a blur.*

This raises further questions about how their training is kept up-to-date and CPD managed across all these roles as well as what weighting is given to each identity. Therefore, not only is there no mandatory requirement for ongoing training for SENCOs, but there is also no formal requirement for a refresher extended programme of learning for those in post more than five years. For example, safeguarding involves regular training to ensure the latest guidelines and legislation are in place. Whilst this may feed into the SENCO role, the connection isn't always evident or explicit. A few SENCOs expressed agency

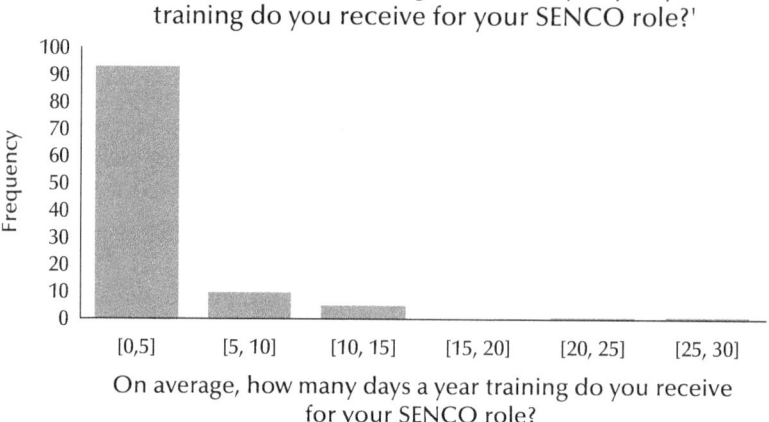

*Figure 14.1* Responses from the questionnaire indicating allocated CPD time, which may include their designated CPD time as teachers [n = 110] (Devi, 2022)

over their professional development, in that they were able to make requests as the need arose. What was not seen was a strategic approach to SENCO development.

In responding to the above question in Figure 14.1, SENCOS were not able to articulate clearly what part of their training specifically related to their SENCO role. Should they have the five teacher inset days plus one SENCO day or should one of the five days be about SENCOs receiving training externally for themselves?

## Content of continuous professional development

Beyond the SENCO induction qualification, SENCOs report an ad hoc approach to professional development with most SENCOs attending courses to do with various needs (dyslexia, autism, mental health etc.). Thus, reverting to a diagnostics approach and homing in on 'specialisms' as opposed to strategic leadership. This results in a more transactional leadership model, as opposed to a transformational one. Hauserman and Stick (2013, p. 186) suggest that many of the 'managerial characteristics of transactional leadership must be present before transformational attributes can emerge'.

For some, the Advanced SENCO Award was considered as a possible useful route. However:

> I did that [induction] qualification, and something called the Advanced SENCO, which was again, if I had had a little more time to have researched, I wouldn't have done those courses.

*I would have done something else because the Advanced SENCO was basically just a repetition of the SENCO award, so it was just another essay.*
— SENCO I2

*I did speak to my head about doing the Advanced SENCO award ... I'm not sure really [what it will bring to my leadership].*
— SENCO I17

During my research, when asked what would be on their professional development wish list, comments ranged from 'anything' (I know nothing) to 'nothing' (I do not need anything). Overwhelmingly, the majority sought needs-based, specialist knowledge training. Only a small group of participants felt some form of leadership training would be helpful. Most were seeking training to enhance their status, believing that this would influence their agency. Yet they were unable to define the link between status and agency.

*You know I just do the things I like to do. And I'm not sure a career path is the right model. I think it's more about improving the status ... It's that idea of you need to have the status elsewhere so that people go oh right oh yeah, we understand that.*
— SENCO I13

*I suppose to me the Master's was the next obvious choice, but you see that wasn't directed by the school. ... I know SENCOs that have used that qualification to then go and become dyslexic assessors, tutors, and that sort of thing.*
— SENCO I14

*You can move on to be assistant head or head. You could progress to a larger school and be non-teaching SENCO.*
— SENCO Q39

*Good for whole-school overview. Next step for me would be assistant head or specialising in specific need.*
— SENCO Q98

This implies most SENCOs recognised the need for more training but hadn't necessarily made the link to how this can help them train others to promote inclusion and distribute the responsibility of SEND across the organisation. In the main, they were still operating in transactional leadership and from a place of unstable identity and self-seeking gratification.

### Preferred delivery method of CPD

CPD delivery methods vary and affect both time commitment (including travel) and cost. Kennedy (2005) proposed a schema of nine different continuous professional development models. Using a multiple choice format in the questionnaire, an extended version of Kennedy (2005) was presented to SENCOs, and they were asked which method would support their professional development against the 12 tasks of a SENCO, as defined in Regulation 50 (Table 14.1). This was undertaken using a thematic approach (see Chapter 3). With the exception of developing their skills in liaising with parents, all SENCOs commented face-to-face training was their preferred option overall. It was unclear if this represents a need to connect, given that so many reference the role as isolating (Mackenzie, 2013, Curran et al., 2018, 2019, 2021), or whether this reflects the relational side of SENCOs. What was of interest was that in relation to promoting inclusion across the school, 'training and cascade' by an external body took greater preference over 'experience'. Possibly suggesting a lack of agency and power. Conversely, experience was rated highly in relation to administration and relationships with parents and carers, i.e. the best method for the administration element of the role is 'learning on the job'. Administration and liaising with parents, SENCOs often refer to the role as time-consuming (Curran et al., 2021; Curran & Boddison, 2021). In my study, both were identified as the areas where most of their time is dedicated. Except for administration, there were no significant differences between a face-to-face community of practice (Wegner et al., 2002) and one that is facilitated online. Wedell (2018) argues the online SENCO forum is the most cost-effective professional development for SENCOs. There is no data pertaining to engagement, and it is possible some SENCOs might consider social media platforms (closed and open) a useful online community of practice. One of the challenges with closed groups using social media platforms is that support is heavily reliant on peer interactions. However, if SENCOs are not engaging in any thought-out continuous professional development beyond the induction qualification, then it is a hit-and-miss process as to the quality and accuracy of support, as well as open to misdirection, based on local variance and the initial prompt provided.

## What is the incentive for CPD? Pay or career trajectory?

### Pay progression for SENCOs

Whilst the last few years have seen significant changes to teachers' pay and conditions (Green, 2016), teachers still have opportunities to progress through a nationally stated and locally determined pay scale. Likewise, those employed with leadership contracts can also progress through the leadership pay scale. Both are based on evidence-based merit and impact. However, though the SENCO is required to be a qualified teacher, there is no currently defined pay progression structure for SENCOs. Some are paid additional TLRs, others receive SEN points. There is variance in these in terms of contract conditions, further progress opportunities and actual value.

## DIMENSION 7: SENCO CPD

Table 14.1 Top preferences for CPD delivery in relation to thematic Regulation 50 based on Kennedy (2005) in Devi (2022)

| SENCO role<br>CPD method | **Theme 1:** Relationship liaison with parents and carers (points 1 and 6) | **Theme 2:** Identification, coordinating and monitoring of provision (points 2 and 3) | **Theme 3:** Record-keeping, information management and reporting (points 4, 5, 7 and 12) | **Theme 4:** Training support staff and teachers (points 9 and 11) | **Theme 5:** Advising teachers (point 10) | **Outlier:** Promoting inclusion across the school (point 8) |
|---|---|---|---|---|---|---|
| *Experience (diving in)* | Preferred | | | | Preferred | Preferred |
| *Training face-to-face* | | Preferred | | Preferred | | |
| *Cascade (local authority or trust)* | | | Preferred | | | |

> *Promises of making the SENCO SLT have been made but nothing has happened as yet. My TLR is only £2500, and I work an additional 20hrs a week. However, I have made wider connections through networking and invited to join panels and groups within the LA. Prior to becoming a SENCO I was an AST [advanced skills teacher] and worked on initial teacher training for 6yrs. I am actively seeking a new post in order to have progression.*
>
> – SENCO Q4

Others are stuck at the top of the teaching pay scale,

> *I am at the top of my pay scale. Not leadership scale. Not SLT. No career progression in current setting – role regarded as middle leadership. Very few SENDCos in my LA as SLT. No incentives for retention.*
>
> – SENCO Q41

For some, CPD is leveraged to justify a pay increase. However, this is down to local variance and local variance can be both at the school level (Garner, 2001; Tissot, 2013) and the local authority level. This SENCO argues the local authority variance and influence to be:

> *Variable. I have worked for two different LAs as SENCo and the current is definitely more supportive, proactive and given the proper level of importance.*
>
> – SENCO Q52

## Career Trajectory

Defining a career trajectory is complex, as progress and success are subjective terms. The construct of a career pathway was seen as either non-existent or alien by most SENCOs. What was not covered in my research in depth is the reward for progression. So intrinsic motivation was assumed as a professional premise.

> *Career pathway, it's funny to think what a career pathway would be for a SENCO. Any SENCO that I've known that have moved on from being a SENCO have gone on to be, so one recently has gone on to be a communication and advisory teacher in another area. So, I see the career pathway of a SENCO as not being a SENCO anymore if you see what I mean, using that knowledge to move on.*
>
> – SENCO I8

# DIMENSION 7: SENCO CPD

The evidence also highlights a brain drain of expertise into the specialist and independent sectors. Thereby challenging the very premise of leadership for the promotion of inclusion.

> *In my school, there is no career progression. I'm self-taught and have expertise due to the training I have selected and paid for myself over the years as well as my [wider] experience in schools. I feel at a disadvantage in the independent sector as no one provides guidance for us.*
> 
> *– SENCO I84*

> *I have progressed from SENCO to assistant head. I have had opportunities to move into [a] special school, but no further progression in mainstream based on SENCO experience.*
> 
> *– SENCO Q95*

## It's not all doom and gloom!

As part of the research (Devi, 2022), SENCOs identified four characteristics for a SENCO career pathway and three principles to design a new way of working. This was to ensure flexibility and to avoid a 'one size fits all model' like the SENCO induction qualification (Table 14.2).

> *Most of the learning of the position comes from 'diving in' and learning on the job as you go, which is good in some respects and can be a good way to learn, but in other ways sometimes you look back and think, I wish someone had told me that or I'd had that training. I think the amount of career progression, comes down to the individual and how much they seek out opportunities and development.*
> 
> *– SENCO Q49*

Applying choice, transparency and a collaborative approach – what this might look like in practice? Here's a suggestion:

*The SLT determines the strategic development for the school and the SENCO is asked for their input in terms of what this would mean for staff development and their own professional development. Funds are allocated to the professional development of the SENCO. In collaboration with the CPD co-ordinator, they choose the best option in*

*Table 14.2* SENCO career pathway characteristics and principles for shaping such a pathway to build in flexibility (Devi, 2022)

| SENCO career pathway characteristics to enhance identity, agency and influence of SENCOs | Principles to shape both the design and usage of a SENCO career pathway |
|---|---|
| 1. CPD that enhances strategic leadership skills and contributions to the setting.<br>2. Stronger and more defined links to teaching and learning leadership.<br>3. Bespoke coaching and mentoring by experienced colleagues.<br>4. Further qualifications (beyond the induction qualification) to enhance status. | A) *Choice* of CPD options.<br>B) *Transparency* of SENCO development through Regulation 51, i.e. annual publication of the SEN Information Report. It was perceived this could aid accountability.<br>C) *Collaboration* where there are challenges. The evolution of MATs is generating more SENCO collaboration; however, in some cases, these networks have become 'echo chambers' for corporate messages, and the local area networks tend to focus on paperwork and processes. Networks that focus on strategic leadership are few and far between. |

terms of having impacts. The training is shared and cascaded in school and through the annual SEN Information Report; there is transparency as to what training the SENCO has attended and why.

As a coherent formula (**within the wider strategic development of the school**), this could look like Figure 14.2.

 **Case study:**

SLIM audit

*Sam is a SENCO who has successfully completed the NASENCO (induction SENCO qualification). Sam has been a SENCO for four years and teaching for seven. In effect, Sam is in the 'professional' stage of the SENCO trajectory (see Figure 4.3 in Chapter 4). Together with Sam's line manager, they evaluate Sam's SEND leadership scores*

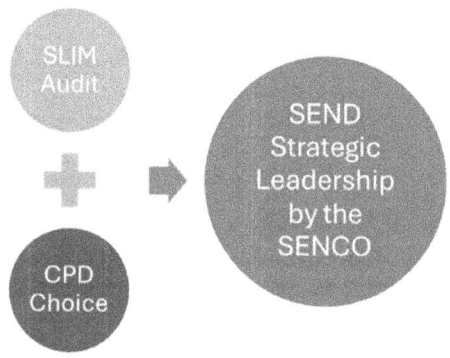

*Figure 14.2* Connecting SLIM to CPD to make informed choices for SENCO strategic leadership development

Devi, 2022

# DIMENSION 7: SENCO CPD

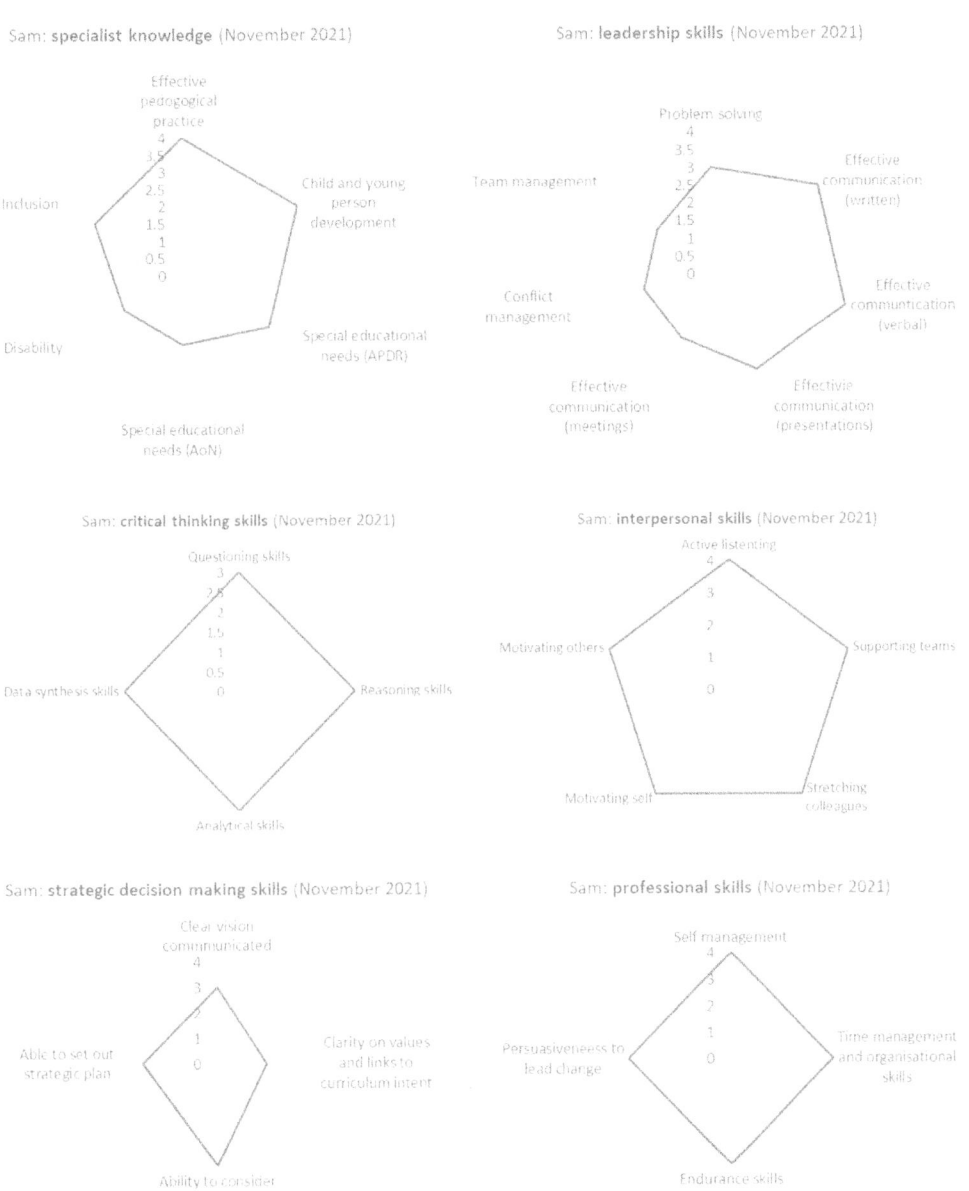

*Figure 14.3* Using SLIM to evaluate Sam (fictitious case study) using spider charts in Devi (2022)

using the SLIM model. For each subattribute, Sam can score a maximum of five. The school has expanded on one dimension to break down communication into different types. Sam can also provide supporting evidence from school activities or outside interests where Sam demonstrates leadership. Sam's self and collaborative scoring is given

*Table 14.3* Using SLIM to evaluate Sam (fictitious case study) in Devi (2022)

| | | score/5 | | | | score/5 | |
|---|---|---|---|---|---|---|---|
| Specialist knowledge | Effective pedogogical practice | 4 | | Leadership skills | Problem solving | 3 | |
| | Child and young person development | 4 | | | Effective communication (written) | 4 | |
| | Special educational needs (APDR) | 3 | | | Effective communtication (verbal) | 4 | |
| | Special educational needs (AON) | 2 | | | Effectivie communication (presentations) | 3 | |
| | Disability | 2 | | | Effective communication (meetings) | 2 | |
| | Inclusion | 3 | | | Conflict management | 2 | |
| | | | | | Team management | 2 | |
| | Total | 18 | Out of 30 | | Total | 20 | Out of 35 |

| | | score/5 | | | | score/5 | |
|---|---|---|---|---|---|---|---|
| Critical thinking skills | Questioning skills | 3 | | Interpersonal skills | Active listening | 4 | |
| | Reasoning skills | 3 | | | Supporting teams | 4 | |
| | Analytical skills | 3 | | | Stretching colleagues | 4 | |
| | Data synthesis skills | 3 | | | Motivating self | 4 | |
| | | | | | Motivating others | 4 | |
| | Total | 12 | Out of 20 | | Total | 20 | Out of 25 |

| | | score/5 | | | | score/5 | |
|---|---|---|---|---|---|---|---|
| Strategic decision making skills | Clear vision commmunicated | 3 | | Professional skills | Self management | 4 | |
| | Clarity on values and links to curriculum intent | 2 | | | Time management and organisational skills | 4 | |
| | Ability to consider options and select | 4 | | | Endurance skills | 4 | |
| | Able to set out strategic plan | 3 | | | Persuasi vene ess to lead change | 4 | |
| | Total | 12 | Out of 20 | | Total | 16 | Out of 20 |

| | Totals | Max |
|---|---|---|
| Specialist knowledge | 18 | 30 |
| Leadership skills | 20 | 35 |
| Critical thinking skills | 12 | 20 |
| Interpersonal skills | 20 | 25 |
| Strategic decision making skills | 12 | 20 |
| Professional skills | 16 | 20 |
| | 98 | 150 |

*in Table 14.3. This provides a total score to reflect overall effectiveness and Figure 14.3 presents the information as six radar charts.*

*Sam has strengths in crucial thinking skills, interpersonal skills and professional skills. Areas of development include some aspects of specialist knowledge, leadership skills and strategic decision-making. Discussions with Sam's line manager reveal that if Sam works on strategic decision-making skills, in particular, links to curriculum intent, this may enhance leadership skills and wider specialist knowledge. It is agreed that Sam should access some CPD. In choosing the most suitable CPD, Sam's line manager and Sam consider the purpose, impact and best delivery method using the CPD options (see Table 14.3), which is an adaptation of Kennedy (2005) used in Devi (2022). This provides Sam with 39 options for CPD delivery plus using definitions from the SEND Code of Practice (Department for Education/Department of Health, 2015, p. 68) three levels of expertise – awareness, enhanced and specialist. Pre-CPD outcomes are agreed between Sam and Sam's line manager. As part of Sam's appraisal process, a re-evaluation takes place to see*

# DIMENSION 7: SENCO CPD

*Table 14.4* Thirty-nine options for CPD delivery based on an extended model of Kennedy (2005)

| Delivery style | | Delivery method | | |
| --- | --- | --- | --- | --- |
| | | Face-to-face | Online | Blended |
| 1 | Training | | | |
| 2 | Award bearing, e.g. master's | | | |
| 3 | Cascade (local authority or trust) | | | |
| 3 | Standards-based, e.g. risk assessment | | | |
| 4 | In-house coaching | | | |
| 5 | External Coaching | | | |
| 6 | In-house mentoring (school or MAT) | | | |
| 7 | External mentoring | | | |
| 8 | Community of practice | | | |
| 9 | Action research | | | |
| 10 | Transformative, e.g. school improvement | | | |
| 11 | Experience (diving in) | | | |
| 12 | Modelling | | | |
| 13 | Other | | | |

*if the CPD has made a difference. If affirmative, it is a celebration. If not, then further dialogue may support the best way forward.*

## CPD choices

SLIM (Devi, 2022) could therefore act as a policy technology (Ball, 2008) to reduce variance and dominance (Ball et al., 2012) between schools, MATs and local authorities by positioning CPD and professional learning communities (Watson, 2014) around SENCO development and using it as a stimulus for growth dialogue. Table 14.4 extends Kennedy (2005) to provide 39 CPD format options. SENCOs, having discussed with their line managers which skills they need to develop, could then choose the most suitable CPD methodology to meet their needs (Deshini et al., 2021). A similar approach could be applied across MATs or at the local authority level to define the content of their professional learning communities (Watson, 2014) or SENCO forums. This approach would ensure that CPD is intentional, both in terms of content and delivery.

*Sam agreed with his line manager to focus on strategic decision-making skills. They considered the best CPD options available and decided to adopt a mixture of external coaching (six sessions across the year) plus number 13 (Other, in Table 14.4), which they defined as three days shadowing the SLT lead for teaching and learning. At the end of the year, Sam's learning and development were evaluated again using SLIM (Devi, 2022). He had made significant progress and could evidence this. However, school circumstances and priorities had changed. Within the new evolving dynamic context, interpersonal skills (which had previously been Sam's strength) now needed some additional input due to circumstances beyond the school's control.*

*SLIM enabled Sam to evaluate himself year after year even though situations were changing. Any CPD provided was purpose-driven. Sam felt he had choice and there was transparency and internal collaboration with an SLT member.*

*Two years later, Sam decided to apply to another school to be a SENCO as a member of the senior leadership team. As part of the application process, Sam shared the SEND leadership scores over the previous years, along with a list of CPD Sam had attended and what difference this has made. For the new school recruiting Sam, SLIM gave them a clear model to evaluate Sam's ability to contribute to their school. For the school losing Sam, they were able to write a JD/PD that best suited their situation at the time. The interview process also gave them clarity on how they could support the new incoming SENCO, who was less experienced than Sam but had new ideas.*

Action task:

- What is your takeaway from Sam's story?
- How could you use SLIM and the CPD choices grid in your setting?
- What's your next step?

Further reading:

*Check out the SEND Code of Practice (DfE, 2015, p. 68) three levels of expertise – awareness, enhanced and specialist.*

Question:

What are your top three takeaways from this chapter?

## Summary

This chapter demonstrated how SLIM (Devi, 2022) can be used to evaluate current practice and define growth. However, CPD is a vital component, and for this, 39 possible models have been shared.

In the final coda, I discuss the relevance of all that has been discussed to you the reader and the wider sector.

PART 3

# Final coda

I hope this book has challenged your believing, thinking and doing.

For me, the SEND Leader Integrated Model (SLIM) is just the beginning of a bigger tidal wave that needs to take place at different levels. As a sector insider, I believe a significant part of my contribution has been to ask the right questions and join the dots between existing paradigms and research.

Action tasks:

1. Go back and read my introductions to Parts 1 and 2 – they cover the why, the how and the so what?
2. Consider how you would use the downloadable materials without compromising copyright integrity.
3. Get in touch. I'd love to hear your thoughts and grow from your understanding too.

*PhD research is designed to add to the body of knowledge. So, let me conclude by stating what I believe I have added to the sector.*

> *The 'hope' I envisage this book provides you, the reader, is three-fold for both SENCOs and their line managers.*
>
> *SENCOs*
>
> *1) You are able to define what an in-role career trajectory looks like.*
> *2) You can use the SLIM model to evaluate your strengths and areas of development, year on year.*
> *3) You intentionally consider the full range of CPD options to advance your career.*
>
> *Line manager*
>
> *1) You invest thought and time into the recruitment and retention of SENCOs.*
> *2) You have meaningful conversations with your SENCO about what's working and what could be even better.*
> *3) You support SENCOs to make wide CPD choices on a regular basis.*

DOI: 10.4324/9781003500131-17

## 7 DIMENSIONS OF HIGHLY EFFECTIVE SENCOS

My broader contribution to the body of knowledge is seven-fold.

1. My research is the first study to address the CPD of SENCO beyond the induction qualification. This builds on the work of previous researchers who have considered the efficacy of the award (Griffiths & Dubsky, 2012; Brown & Doveston, 2014; Passy et al., 2017). However, it is the only research (to my knowledge) that has focused on Regulation 50 (Children & Families Act, 2014) as a basis for understanding the role of the SENCO.
2. In undertaking this research, I have explored the transition from teacher identity to SENCO identity by considering the construct of teams for inclusion (Robinson, 2017) that embrace different practitioners at different stages of their careers. This has led to my third contribution.
3. The creation of a conceptual framework that combines the individual, the sector, the organisation and the prospects for the SENCO.
4. I have put forward a career trajectory for SENCOs aspiring to be on the senior leadership team. This embraces the work of Trent (2011) and Tissot (2013).
5. For those not aspiring to senior leadership, I have defined attributes that would frame a CPD pathway embracing choice and wider system contributions. I believe my most significant contribution is number six.
6. The SEND Leader Integrated Model (SLIM), with six domains that help shape the identity of a SENCO combining connected (Hayward & Newman, 2014) and transformational leadership (Bass, 1990; Hauserman & Stick, 2013; Jensen et al., 2018) so that there is greater distributed leadership of SEND in schools and a focus on socio-moral connectedness (Wanjiru, 2021).
7. Finally, I have demonstrated that the lever for SENCO agency is best achieved when used in conjunction with dialogues on CPD (Miller et al., 2016) to develop an organic leader (King, 2012). In other words, SENCOs shape the system by developing themselves (Sherman & Teemant, 2021) to increase influence (power).

When I started my research, I knew choice needed to be a key part of any defined pathway beyond the mandatory induction qualification. I also knew that the sector needed a more structured approach to choosing CPD options, particularly in terms of delivery models. The bridge between these two notions is the SLIM, as shown in Figure F.1.

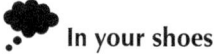 **In your shoes:**

My final questions:

- **At the setting level**: SENCOs, line managers and governors, how would you apply the content of this book to your context? What would you do differently, and what needs to change?
- **At the multi-academy trust level**: What are the implications for SENCOs in your trust, especially in terms of CPD and career progression opportunities?

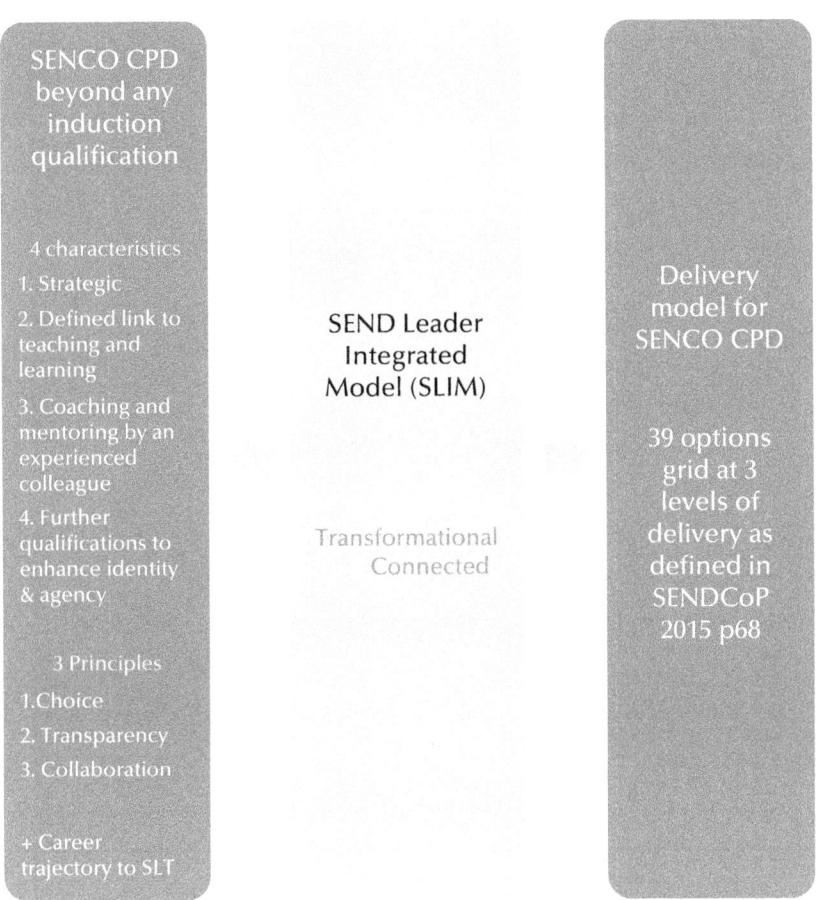

*Figure F.1* Visual connectivity schema of SENCO career trajectory, the SEND leadership model and modes of CPD delivery

- **At the national level**: Maybe it is time to think about and deliver support for SENCOs differently. What are your thoughts? Let's keep talking together as a sector committed to improving the working lives of SENCOs. Avoid the quick fixes and focus on long-term foundational growth.

Thank you for being part of the change processes needed in the sector.

# References

Agathangelou, S., Charalambous, C., & Koutselini, M. (2016). Reconsidering the contribution of teacher knowledge to student learning: Linear or curvilinear effects? *Teaching and Teacher Education*, 57, 125–138.

Anderson, J., Boyle, C., & Deppeler, J. (2014). The ecology of inclusive education reconceptualising Bronfenbrenner. In H. Zhang, P. Wing Keung Chan, & C. Boyle (Eds.), *Equality in education: Fairness and inclusion* (pp. 23–34). Rotterdam: Sense.

Bačáková, M., & Closs, A. (2013). Continuing professional development (CPD) as a means to reducing barriers to inclusive education: Research study of the education of refugee children in the Czech Republic. *European Journal of Special Needs Education*, 28(2), 203–216.

Ball, S., Maguire, M., Braun, A., Perryman, J., & Hoskins, K. (2012). Assessment technologies in schools: 'Deliverology' and the 'play of dominations'. *Research Papers in Education*, 27(5), 513–533.

Ball, S. J. (2008). *The education debate: Politics and policy in the 21st century*. Bristol: Policy Press.

Banegas, D., & Gerlach, D. (2021). Critical language teacher education: A duoethnography of teacher educators' identities and agency. *System (Linköping)*, 98, 102474.

Bass, B. (1990). From transactional to transformational leadership: Learning to share the vision. *Organizational Dynamics*, 18(3), 19–31.

Beauchamp, C., & Thomas, L. (2009). Understanding teacher identity: An overview of issues in the literature and implications for teacher education. *Cambridge Journal of Education*, 39(2), 175–189.

Boswell, N., & Woods, K. (2021). Facilitators and barriers of co-production of services with children and young people within education, health, and care services. *Educational and Child Psychology*, 38(2), 41–52.

Bower, K. (2020). School leaders' perspectives on content and language integrated learning in England. *Language, Culture, and Curriculum*, 33(4), 351–367.

Bristol, L. (2015). Leading-for-inclusion: Transforming action through teacher talk. *International Journal of Inclusive Education*, 19(8), 802–820.

# REFERENCES

Brown, J., & Doveston, M. (2014). Short sprint or an endurance test: The perceived impact of the national award for special educational needs coordination. *Teacher Development*, 18(4), 495–510.

Brueggemann, W. (1997). *Cadences of home: Preaching among exiles*. Louisville, KY: Westminster John Knox Press.

Bryman, A. (2016). *Social research methods* (5th ed.). Oxford: Oxford University Press.

Buchanan, R. (2015). Teacher identity and agency in an era of accountability. *Teachers and Teaching, Theory and Practice*, 21(6), 700–719.

Carter, A. (2015). Carter review of initial teacher training (ITT) commissioned by the Secretary of State, DfE. https://assets.publishing.service.gov.uk/government/uploads/system/uploads/attachment_data/file/399957/Carter_Review.pdf

Castro, S., & Palikara, O. (2016). Mind the gap: The new special educational needs and disability legislation in England. *Frontiers in Education (Lausanne)*, 1, Frontiers in education (Lausanne), 2016-11-01. https://doi.org/10.3389/feduc.2016.00004

Chetty, R., Friedman, J., & Rockoff, J. (2014). Measuring the impacts of teachers, [part] II: Teacher value-added and student outcomes in adulthood. *The American Economic Review*, 104(9), 2633–2679.

Clapp-Smith, R., Hammond, M., Lester, G., & Palanski, M. (2019). Promoting identity development in leadership education: A multidomain approach to developing the whole leader. *Journal of Management Education*, 43(1), 10–34.

Clark, C. (2017). Action research to improve phonological recognition at Key Stage 1 with reference to pupils with special educational needs. *Support for Learning*, 32(4), 337–351.

Clarke, M. (2009). The ethico-politics of teacher identity. *Educational Philosophy and Theory*, 41(2), 185–200.

Coe, R., Aloisi, C., Higgins, S., & Major, L. E. (2014). *What makes great teaching? review of the underpinning research*. Project Report. London: Sutton Trust.

Cohen, N., & Arieli, T. (2011). Field research in conflict environments: Methodological challenges and snowball sampling. *Journal of Peace Research*, 48(4), 423–435.

Coldwell, M. (2017). Exploring the influence of professional development on teacher careers: A path model approach. *Teaching and Teacher Education*, 61, 189–198.

Cole, B. (2005). Mission impossible? Special educational needs, inclusion, and the re-conceptualization of the role of the SENCO in England and Wales. *European Journal of Special Needs Education*, 20(3), 287–307.

Copeland, A. H. (1945). Review of 'The Theory of Games and Economic Behavior'. *Bulletin of the American Mathematical Society*, 51, 498–504. https://doi.org/10.1090/s0002-9904-1945-08391-8

# REFERENCES

Cordingley, P., Higgins, S., Greany, T., et al. (2015). *Developing great teaching: Lessons from the international reviews into effective professional development.* London: Teacher Development Trust. http://TDTrust.org/dgt

Covey, S. (2004). *The 7 habits of highly effective people.* London: Simon & Schuster UK.

Curran, H. (2019). 'The SEND code of practice has given me clout': A phenomenological study illustrating how SENCos managed the introduction of the SEND reforms. *British Journal of Special Education*, 46(1), 76–93.

Curran, H., & Boddison, A. (2021). 'It's the best job in the world, but one of the hardest, loneliest, most misunderstood roles in a school.' Understanding the complexity of the SENCO role post-SEND reform. *Journal of Research in Special Educational Needs*, 21(1), 39–48.

Curran, H., Boddison, A., & Moloney, H. (2021). *National SENCO workforce survey 2020: Supporting children and young people with special educational needs and their families during the coronavirus (COVID–19) pandemic.* Bath Spa University and nasen, Bath.

Curran, H., Moloney, H., Heavy, A., & Boddison, A. (2018). *It's about time: The impact of SENCO workload on the professional and the school.* Bath Spa University, nasen, NEU.

Curran, H., Moloney, H., Heavy, A., & Boddison, A. (2019). *The time is now: Addressing missed opportunities for special educational needs support and coordination in our schools.* Bath Spa University, nasen, NEU.

Day, C., Kington, A., Stobart, G., & Sammons, P. (2006). The personal and professional selves of teachers: Stable and unstable identities. *British Educational Research Journal*, 32(4), 601–616.

Day, C., Sammons, P., Stobart, G., Kington, A., & Gu, Q. (2007). *Teachers matter: Connecting lives, work, and effectiveness.* Maidenhead: Open University Press.

DeLuca, C. (2012). Promoting inclusivity through and within teacher education programmes. *Journal of Education for Teaching: JET*, 38(5), 551–569.

Department for Education (DfE) (2012). Teachers' standards. https://www.gov.uk/government/publications/teachers-standards

Department for Education (2014). Promoting fundamental British values as part of SMSC in schools. https://assets.publishing.service.gov.uk/government/uploads/system/uploads/attachment_data/file/380595/SMSC_Guidance_Maintained_Schools.pdf

Department for Education (2018). Induction for newly qualified teachers (NQTs). https://www.gov.uk/government/publications/induction-for-newly-qualified-teachers-nqts (accessed November 2020)

Department for Education (2021a). Induction for early career teachers (England). https://www.gov.uk/government/publications/induction-for-early-career-teachers-england (accessed April 2021)

# REFERENCES

Department for Education (2024). *Special educational needs in England.* https://explore-education-statistics.service.gov.uk/find-statistics/special-educational-needs-in-england

Department for Education/Department of Health (2015). *Special educational needs and disability code of practice: 0 to 25 years.* www.gov.uk/government/publications/send-codeof-practice-0-to-25

Deshini, P., Govender, S., & Dorasamy, N. (2021). Leaderships' handling of conflict in schools in the Phoenix circuit. *International Journal of Entrepreneurship*, 25, 1–9.

Devi, A., & Bowers, J. (2022). *Journeying to the heart of SENCO Wellbeing.* London: Routledge

Devi, A., & Jaggar, S. (2025). *Neuroplasticity and neurodiversity in the classroom.* London: Critical Publishing.

Devi, A. (2016). *Take Time – time management strategies and case studies for SENCOs* [eBook]. London: Optimus Publishing.

Devi, A. (2020). (Series Editor Hollis, E.) *Essential guides for early career teachers: Special educational needs and disability.* London: Critical Publishing.

Devi, A. (2022). SENCOs in England: Career trajectory, CPD and a leadership model through identity and agency (PhD Thesis), Lancaster University.

Dickie-Clark, Hamish F. (1966). The marginal situation: A contribution to marginality theory. *Social Forces*, 44(3), 363–370.

Dobson, G. (2019). Understanding the SENCo workforce: Re-examination of selected studies through the lens of an accurate national dataset. *British Journal of Special Education*, 46(4), 445–464.

Dobson, G., & Douglas, G. (2020a). Who would do that role? Understanding why teachers become SENCos through an ecological systems theory. *Educational Review (Birmingham)*, 72(3), 298–318.

Dobson, G., & Douglas, G. (2020b). Factors influencing the career interest of SENCOs in English schools. *British Educational Research Journal*, 46(6), 1256–1278.

Docherty, R. (2019). Personalizing education: A person-centred approach for children with special educational needs. *Educational Psychology in Practice*, 35(2), 239–240.

Doka, K. J. 1989. *Disenfranchised grief: Recognising hidden human sorrow.* Lexington, KY: Lexington Books.

Done, E., Murphy, M., & Bedford, C. (2016a). Change management and the SENCo role: Developing key performance indicators of inclusivity. *Support for Learning*, 31(1), 13–26.

Done, L., Murphy, M., & Watt, M. (2016b). Change management and the SENCo role: Developing key performance indicators in the strategic development of inclusivity. *Support for Learning*, 31(4), 281–295.

Essex, J., Alexiadou, N., & Zwozdiak-Myers, P. (2019). Understanding inclusion in teacher education – a view from student teachers in England. *International*

*Journal of Inclusive Education*, 25(12), 1425–1442. https://doi.org/10.1080/1360 3116.2019.1614232

Eteläpelto, A., Vähäsantanen, K., & Hökkä, P. (2015). How do novice teachers in Finland perceive their professional agency? *Teachers and Teaching, Theory and Practice*, 21(6), 660–680.

Farrow, J., Wasik, B., & Hindman, A. (2020). Exploring the unique contributions of teachers' syntax to pre-schoolers' and kindergarteners' vocabulary learning. *Early Childhood Research Quarterly*, 51, 178–190.

Forlin, C. (Ed.) (2010). *Reframing teacher education for inclusion*. London: Routledge.

Forlin, C. (Ed.) (2012). *Future directions for inclusive teacher education: An international perspective*. London: Routledge.

Garner, P. (2001). What is the weight of a badger? Teachers experiences of working with children with learning difficulties. In J. Wearmouth (Ed.), *Special educational needs in the context of inclusion* (pp. 119–136). London: David Fulton.

Gavish, B. (2017). Four profiles of inclusive supportive teachers: Perceptions of their status and role in implementing inclusion of students with special needs in general classrooms. *Teaching and Teacher Education*, 61, 37–46.

Goleman, D. (2005). *Emotional intelligence*. New York: Bantam Books.

Gov.uk Children and Families Act 2014 - Part 3 (Children and young people in England with Special Educational Needs or Disabilities. https://www.legislation.gov.uk/ukpga/2014/6/part/3

Gov.uk The Education (Special Educational Needs Co-ordinators) (England) Regulations 2008. https://www.legislation.gov.uk/uksi/2008/2945/made

Green, J. (2016). Listening as leadership. *Schools (Chicago, Ill.)*, 13(2), 211–225.

Griffiths, D., & Dubsky, R. (2012). Evaluating the impact of the new National Award for SENCos: Transforming landscapes or gardening in a gale? *British Journal of Special Education*, 39(4), 164–172.

Hallett, F. (2021). Can SENCOs do their job in a bubble? The impact of Covid-19 on the ways in which we conceptualise provision for learners with special educational needs. *Oxford Review of Education*, 48(2), 1–13.

Hallett, F., & Hallett, G. (2010). *Transforming the role of the Senco*. Berkshire: McGraw-Hill Education.

Hauserman, C., & Stick, S. (2013). The leadership teachers want from principals: Transformational. *Canadian Journal of Education*, 36(3), 184–203.

Havik, T., & Westergård, E. (2020). Do teachers matter? Students' perceptions of classroom interactions and student engagement. *Scandinavian Journal of Educational Research*, 64(4), 488–507. https://doi.org/10.1080/00313831.2019.1577754

Hayward, S., & Newman, M. (2014). Connected leadership. *Training Journal*, 55.

Holland, D. C., Lachicotte, W., Jr, Skinner, D., & Cain, C. (1998). *Identity and agency in cultural worlds*. Harvard University Press. https://www.infoamerica.org/documentos_pdf/holland02.pdf

# REFERENCES

Holland, D., & Lachicotte, W. (2007). Vygotsky, Mead, and the new sociocultural studies of identity. In H. Daniels, M. Cole, & J. V. Wertsch (Eds.), *The Cambridge companion to Vygotsky* (pp. 101–135). Cambridge: Cambridge University Press. https://doi.org/10.1017/CCOL0521831040.005

Hughes, M. (2002). *Tweak to transform: Improving teaching: A practical handbook for school leaders*. Stafford: Network Continuum Education.

Jeffrey, B., & Troman, G. (2013). Managing creative teaching and performative practices. *Thinking Skills and Creativity*, 9, 24–34.

Jensen, U., Moynihan, D., & Salomonsen, H. (2018). Communicating the vision: How face-to-face dialogue facilitates transformational leadership. *Public Administration Review*, 78(3), 350–361.

Jones, L., Dean, C., Dunhill, A., Hope, M., & Shaw, P. (2020). 'We are the same as everyone else just with a different and unique backstory': Identity, belonging and 'othering' within education for young people who are 'looked after.' *Children & Society*, 34(6), 492–506.

Kearns, H. (2005). Exploring the Experiential Learning of Special Educational Needs Coordinators. *Journal of In-service Education*, 31(1), 131–150.

Kemmis, S., & Grootenboer, P. (2008). Situating Praxis in practice. In I. S. Kemmis & T. Smith (Red.), *Enabling Praxis: Challenges for education* (pp. 37–62). Amsterdam: Sense Publishing. [ResearchGate]

Kemmis, S., Wilkinson, J., Edwards-Groves, C., Hardy, I., Grootenboer, P., & Bristol, L. (2013). *Changing practices, changing education* (2014th ed.). Singapore: Springer Singapore Pte. Limited.

Kennedy, A. (2005). Models of continuing professional development: A framework for analysis. *Journal of In-service Education*, 31(2), 235–250.

King, F. (2012). Developing and sustaining teachers' professional learning: A case study of collaborative professional development (Doctoral thesis), University of Lincoln, Lincoln.

Kosnik, C., & Beck, C. (2011). *Teaching in a Nutshell: Navigating your teacher education program as a student teacher*. Abingdon: Routledge.

Kramer, Marlene. (1975). Reality shock: Why nurses leave nursing. *The American Journal of Nursing*, 75(5), 891.

Kuhn, T. S. (1962). *The structure of scientific revolutions*. Chicago: University of Chicago Press.

Kvale, S. (1996). *InterViews: An introduction to qualitative research interviewing*. Thousand Oaks, CA: SAGE.

Lai, L., & Kapstad, J. (2009). Perceived competence mobilization: An explorative study of predictors and impact on turnover intentions. *International Journal of Human Resource Management*, 20(9), 1985–1998.

Lamb, B. (2009). The Lamb Inquiry, commissioned by the department of children's, schools, and families (DCSF). https://www.natsip.org.uk/doc-library-login/lamb-enquiry/104-lamb-inquiry-final-report-dec2009

Layton, L. (2005). Special educational needs coordinators and leadership: A role too far? *Support for Learning*, 20(2), 53–60.

Leadbeater, C. (2016). *The problem solvers*. Pearson. https://www.pearson.com/content/dam/corporate/global/pearson-dot-com/files/learning/Problem-Solvers-Web-.pdf

Leask, M., & Younie, S. (2013). National models for continuing professional development: The challenges of twenty-first-century knowledge management. *Professional Development in Education*, 39(2), 273–287.

Lewis, A., & Ogilvie, M. (2003). Support, knowledge, and identity: Reported gains from involvement in a special email group – the SENCo–Forum. *British Journal of Special Education*, 30(1), 44–50.

Lin, H., Grudnoff, L., & Hill, M. (2021). Navigating personal and contextual factors of SENCo teacher identity. *International Journal of Inclusive Education*, 27(7), 1–15 https://www.researchgate.net/publication/348745530_Navigating_personal_and_contextual_factors_of_SENCo_teacher_identity

Livingston, K. (2016). Developing teachers' and teacher educators' professional identity in changing contexts. *European Journal of Teacher Education*, 39(4), 401–402.

Lyubovnikova, J., Legood, A., Turner, N., & Mamakouka, A. (2017). How authentic leadership influences team performance: The mediating role of team reflexivity. *Journal of Business Ethics*, 141(1), 59–70.

Mackenzie, S. (2007). A review of recent developments in the role of the SENCo in the UK. *British Journal of Special Education*, 34(4), 212–218.

Mackenzie, S. (2013). Achievers, confidence-builders, advocates, relationship-developers, and system-changers: What 'making a difference' means to those who work with children with special educational needs – a typology of rewards. *Teachers and Teaching, Theory and Practice*, 19(4), 433–448.

Makopoulou, K., Penney, D., Neville, R., & Thomas, G. (2019). What sort of 'inclusion' is continuing professional development promoting? An investigation of a national CPD programme for inclusive physical education. *International Journal of Inclusive Education*, 26(3), 245–262. https://doi.org/10.1080/13603116.2019.1647297

Male, D. (1996). Special needs coordinators' career continuation plans. *Support for Learning*, 11(2), 88–92.

Marquet, L. D. (2015). *Turn the ship around!* New York: Portfolio Penguin.

Miller, H. L. (2022). Why empathetic leadership is the most effective leadership style. *Leaders*. https://leaders.com/articles/leadership/empathetic-leadership/ (accessed 14 May 2024)

Miller, R., Goddard, R., Kim, M., Jacob, R., Goddard, Y., & Schroeder, P. (2016). Can professional development improve school leadership? Results from a randomized control trial assessing the impact of McREL's balanced leadership program on principals in rural michigan schools. *Educational Administration Quarterly*, 52(4), 531–566.

# REFERENCES

Mintrop, R., & Zumpe, E. (2019). Solving real-life problems of practice and education leaders' school improvement mind-set. *American Journal of Education*, 125(3), 295–344.

Mintz, J. (2019). A comparative study of the impact of enhanced input on inclusion at pre-service and induction phases on the self-efficacy of beginning teachers to work effectively with children with special educational needs. *British Educational Research Journal*, 45(2), 254–274.

Momeny, L., & Gourgues, M. (2019). Communication that develops: Clarity of process on transformational leadership through study of effective communication of emotional intelligence. *Christian Education Journal*, 16(2), 226–240.

Mumford, M., Todd, E., Higgs, C., & McIntosh, T. (2017). Cognitive skills and leadership performance: The nine critical skills. *The Leadership Quarterly*, 28(1), 24–39.

Murtagh, L. (2017). Invisible perceptions: Understanding the perceptions of university tutors towards trainee teachers with parental responsibilities. *Asia-Pacific Journal of Teacher Education*, 45(4), 383–398.

National Audit Office (2019). Support for pupils with special educational needs and disabilities in England. https://www.nao.org.uk/report/support-for-pupils-with-special-educational-needs-and-disabilities/

Neck, C., & Manz, C. (1992). Thought self-leadership: The influence of self-talk and mental imagery on performance. *Journal of Organizational Behavior*, 13(7), 681–699.

Neck, C., & Milliman, J. (1994). Thought self-leadership: Finding spiritual fulfilment in organizational life. *Journal of Managerial Psychology*, 9(6), 9–16.

Northouse, P. (2019). *Leadership: Theory and practice*. Thousand Oaks, CA: Sage Publications.

O'Toole, J. (1993). *The executive compass*. Oxford: Oxford University Press.

Ofsted (2019) Education Inspection Framework (EIF). https://www.gov.uk/government/publications/education-inspection-framework

Oldham, J., & Radford, J. (2011). Secondary SENCo leadership: A universal or specialist role? *British Journal of Special Education*, 38(3), 126–134.

Olivier, E., Galand, B., Hospel, V., & Dellisse, S. (2020). Understanding behavioural engagement and achievement: The roles of teaching practices and student sense of competence and task value. *British Journal of Educational Psychology*, 90(4), 887–909.

Paiva-Salisbury, M. L., & Schwanz, K. A. (2022). Building compassion fatigue resilience: Awareness, prevention, and intervention for pre-professionals and current practitioners. *Journal of Health Service Psychology*, 48(1), 39–46. https://doi.org/10.1007/s42843-022-00054-9

Papadatou, Danai. (2000). A proposed model of health professionals' grieving process. *OMEGA-Journal of Death and Dying* 41(1), 59–77.

Park, Robert E. (1928). Human migration and the marginal man. *American Journal of Sociology*, 33(6), 881–893.

# REFERENCES

Parker, B., & Bowell, B. (1998). Exploiting computer-mediated communication to support in-service professional development: The SENCO experience. *Journal of Information Technology for Teacher Education, 7*(2), 229–246.

Passy, R., Georgeson, J., Schaefer, N., & Kaimi, I. (2017). *Evaluation of the impact and effectiveness of the national award for special educational needs coordination*. Achievement for All. Newbury: Plymouth University.

Pearson, S. (2008). Deafened by silence or by the sound of footsteps? An investigation of the recruitment, induction, and retention of special educational needs coordinators (SENCOs) in England. *Journal of Research in Special Educational Needs, 8*, 96–110.

Pearson, S., Mitchell, R., & Rapti, M. (2015). 'I will be "fighting" even more for pupils with SEN': SENCOs' role predictions in the changing English policy context. *Journal of Research in Special Educational Needs, 15*(1), 48–56.

Pearson, S., & Ralph, S. (2007). The identity of SENCos: Insights through images. *Journal of Research in Special Educational Needs, 7*(1), 36–45.

Pinnock, R., & Welch, P. (2014). Learning clinical reasoning. *Journal of Paediatrics and Child Health, 50*(4), 253–257.

Plender, A. (2019). *A psychosocial approach exploring the experiences of primary school special educational needs co-ordinators (SENCOs)*. University of Essex & Tavistock and Portman NHS Foundation Trust. https://repository.tavistockandportman.ac.uk/2072/1/Plender%20-%20Psychosocial.pdf

Plowright, D. (2011). *Using mixed methods: frameworks for an integrated methodology*. London: SAGE Publications.

Pratt, M. G., Rockmann, K. W., & Kaufmann, J. B. (2006). Constructing professional identity: The role of work and identity learning cycles in the customization of identity among medical residents. *Academy of Management Journal, 49*(2), 235–262. https://doi.org/10.5465/AMJ.2006.20786060

Pulsford, M. (2020). 'I could have been the caretaker in a suit': Men as primary school SENCos in an era of change. *Education 3–13, 48*(7), 820–832.

Quin, D. (2017). Longitudinal and contextual associations between teacher-student relationships and student engagement: A systematic review. *Review of Educational Research, 87*(2), 345–387.

Quinteiro, P., Passos, A., & Curral, L. (2016). Thought self-leadership and effectiveness in self-management teams. *Leadership (London, England), 12*(1), 110–126.

Quintrell, M., & Maguire, M. (2000). Older and wiser, or just at the end of the line? The perceptions of mature trainee teachers. *Westminster Studies in Education, 23*(1), 19–30.

Qureshi, S. (2014). Herding cats or getting heard: The SENCo-teacher dynamic and its impact on teachers' classroom practice. *Support for Learning, 29*(3), 217–229.

Reeves, J. (2009). Teacher investment in learner identity. *Teaching and Teacher Education, 25*(1), 34–41. https://doi.org/10.1016/j.tate.2008.06.003

Reid, H., & Soan, S. (2019). Providing support to senior managers in schools via 'clinical' supervision: A purposeful, restorative professional and personal developmental space. *Professional Development in Education*, 45(1), 59–72.

Rhoades, B., Greenberg, M., & Domitrovich, C. (2009). The contribution of inhibitory control to pre-schoolers' social–emotional competence. *Journal of Applied Developmental Psychology*, 30(3), 310–320.

Robinson, D. (2017). Effective inclusive teacher education for special educational needs and disabilities: Some more thoughts on the way forward. *Teaching and Teacher Education*, 61, 164–178.

Robinson, J. (2016). 'Outside of everything and everybody': Renegotiating place in the classroom. *Research in Drama Education*, 21(2), 214–228.

Rosen-Webb, S. (2011). Nobody tells you how to be a SENCo. *British Journal of Special Education*, 38(4), 159–168.

Rotter, J. B. (1954). *Social learning and clinical psychology*. New York: Prentice-Hall.

Rushton, G. (2014). From occupation to profession: A perspective on the American association of chemistry teachers. *Journal of Chemical Education*, 91(1), 8–9.

Sammons, P., Day, C., Kington, A., Gu, Q., Stobart, G., & Smees, R. (2007). Exploring variations in teachers' work, lives, and their effects on pupils: Key findings and implications from a longitudinal mixed-method study. *British Educational Research Journal*, 33(5), 681–701.

Sanderson, H., & Lepkowsky, M. B. (2014). *Person-centred teams: A practical guide to delivering personalisation through effective team-work*. London: Jessica Kingsley Publishers.

Saunders, M. (2000). Beginning an evaluation with RUFDATA: Theorizing a practical approach to evaluation planning. *Evaluation (London, England. 1995)*, 6(1), 7–21.

Scutt, C., & Harrison, S. (2019). *Teacher CPD: International trends, opportunities and challenges*. London: Chartered College of Teaching.

Sherman, B., & Teemant, A. (2021). Agency, identity, power: An agentive triad model for teacher action. *Educational Philosophy and Theory*, 1–12. https://doi.org/10.1080/00131857.2021.1929174

Skinner, B., Leavey, G., & Rothi, D. (2021). Managerialism and teacher professional identity: Impact on well-being among teachers in the UK. *Educational Review (Birmingham)*, 73(1), 1–16.

Smart, J. (2013). *Clarity*. West Sussex: Capstone Publishing Ltd.

Smart, J. (2023). *Clarity* (2nd ed.). West Sussex: Capstone Publishing Ltd.

Smith, K., Hodson, E., & Brown, T. (2013). Teacher educator changing perceptions of theory. *Educational Action Research*, 21(2), 237–252.

Smith, M., & Broomhead, K. (2019). Time, expertise, and status: Barriers faced by mainstream primary school SENCos in the pursuit of providing effective provision for children with SEND. *Support for Learning*, 34(1), 54–70.

# REFERENCES

Solberg, S., Edwards, A., & Nyborg, G. (2021). Leading for school inclusion and prevention? How school leadership teams support shy students and their teachers. *Scandinavian Journal of Educational Research*, 65(7), 1203–1216.

Struyvea, C., Hannesb, K., Mereditha, C., Vandecandelaerea, M., Gielenam, S., & De Frainea, B. (2018). Teacher leadership in practice: Mapping the negotiation of the position of the special educational needs coordinator in schools. *Scandinavian Journal of Educational Research*, 62(5), 701.

Szwed, C. (2007). Reconsidering the role of the primary special educational needs co-ordinator: Policy, practice, and future priorities. *British Journal of Special Education*, 34(2), 96–104.

Thorpe, K., Sullivan, V., Jansen, E., McDonald, P., Sumsion, J., & Irvine, S. (2020). A man in the centre: Inclusion and contribution of male educators in early childhood education and care teaching teams. *Early Child Development and Care*, 190(6), 921–934.

Tian, M., Risku, M., & Collin, K. (2016). A meta-analysis of distributed leadership from 2002–2013: Theory development, empirical evidence and future research focus. *Educational Management Administration & Leadership*, 44(1), 146–164.

Tissot, C. (2013). The role of SENCos as leaders. *British Journal of Special Education*, 40(1), 33–40.

Trent, J. (2011). 'Four years on, I'm ready to teach': Teacher education and the construction of teacher identities. *Teachers and Teaching, Theory and Practice*, 17(5), 529–543.

Van der Heijden, H. R. M. A., Beijaard, D., Geldens, J. J. M., & Popeijus, H. L. (2018). Understanding teachers as change agents: An investigation of primary school teachers' self-perception. *Journal of Educational Change*, 19(3), 347–373.

Varghese, M., Morgan, B., Johnston, B., & Johnson, K. A. (2005). Theorizing language teacher identity: Three Perspectives and Beyond. *Journal of Language, Identity & Education*, 4(1), 21–44. https://doi.org/10.1207/s15327701jlie0401_2

von Neumann, J., & Morgenstern, O. (1944). *Theory of games and economic behaviour*. Princeton: Princeton University Press.

Wanjiru, J. (2021). School leadership and post-conflict education: How can their roles in developing inclusive practices in post-conflict schooling be understood and conceptualized? *Educational Management, Administration & Leadership*, 49(1), 145–163.

Watson, C. (2014). Effective professional learning communities? The possibilities for teachers as agents of change in schools. *British Educational Research Journal*, 40(1), 18–29.

Wedell, K. (1999). Points from the SENCo-Forum. *British Journal of Special Education*, 26(1), 54.

Wedell, K. (2002). Points from the SENCo-Forum. *British Journal of Special Education*, 29(2), 101.

Wedell, K. (2012). SENCos supporting each other: The SENCo forum. *Support for Learning*, 27(2), 67–72.

Wedell, K. (2016). Points from the SENCo-Forum. *British Journal of Special Education,* 43(2), 195–198.

Wedell, K. (2018). Points from the SENCo-Forum: The 'Points from the SENCo-forum' column: Its 20th anniversary year. *British Journal of Special Education,* 45(1), 98–101.

Wedell, K. (2019). Points from the SENCo-Forum. *British Journal of Special Education,* 46(3), 379–381.

Wedell, K. (2020). Points from the SENCo-Forum. *British Journal of Special Education,* 47(2), 258–260.

Wenger, E. (1998). *Communities of practice: Learning, meaning, and identity.* Cambridge, Cambridge University Press.

Wenger, E., McDermott, R. A., & Snyder, W. (2002). *Cultivating communities of practice, a guide to managing knowledge.* Boston, MA: Harvard Business School Press.

Wilkinson, S., & Penney, D. (2014). The effects of setting on classroom teaching and student learning in mainstream mathematics, English and science lessons: A critical review of the literature in England. *Educational Review (Birmingham),* 66(4), 411–427.

Williams-Brown, Z., & Hodkinson, A. (2021). 'What is considered good for everyone may not be good for children with Special Educational Needs and Disabilities': Teacher's perspectives on inclusion in England. *Education 3–13,* 49(6), 688–702.

Woolhouse, Clare. (2015). Teachers performing gender and belonging: a case study of how SENCOs narrate inclusion identities. *Gender and Education,* 27. https://doi.org/10.1080/09540253.2014.992300

Wulf, R. (2020). The historical roots of gestalt therapy theory. www.gestalt.org/wulf.htm (accessed 9 April 2024)

Yih, C. (2021). The chaplain grieves in silence: Marginalisation, disenfranchised grief, and chaplaincy. *Practical Theology.* https://doi.org/10.1080/1756073X.2021.1967558

Young, H. (2016). Asking the 'right' questions: The constitution of school governing bodies as apolitical. *Journal of Education Policy,* 31(2), 161–177.

# Index

*Page numbers in **bold** reference tables.

ability 16–17
accountability 18
active listening 109–110, **115**
adaptions, recruiting SENCOs 27–28
administrative efficiency 19–20
Advanced SENCO Award 144
agency 24, 47, 52
analysis, critical thinking skills 99–100, **103**
anchoring identity 40–45
applying for SENCO role **38**
areas of need 72
articulating core values 121–122, **127**
aspirations of SENCOs 57–58
assessment approach 71
authority functions 8–10, 142

bonding capital 53
boredom 123–124
boundaries, relationship boundaries 124–126, **128**

capability 16
capacity 16
capital 53, 130; emotional capital 130–131; human capital 131; social capital 131
career pathway **150**
career trajectory: continuous professional development 148–152; visual connectivity schema of SENCO career trajectory 157
case studies: continuous professional development (CPD) 140, 150–153; core values 122; recruiting SENCOs 28; staying the course 44–45; transition from teacher to SENCO 34–35; transitioning teachers to SENCOs 33–34
change, SENCO's relationship with 17
child and young person development 71–73, **77**
Children and Families Act 2014 3, 75
CL *see* connected leadership
classroom experience 35

colleagues, stretching 112, **116**
communication 19; effective communication 91; leadership skills 87–88
compassion fatigue 41
complacency 123–124
complex needs 72
conceptual framework 50–51
conflict management 88–89; leadership skills **92**
connected leadership (CL) 67, 82, 95, 109; emotional capital 130
content of continuous professional development (CPD) 144–145
continuous professional development (CPD) 18, 138; career trajectory 148–152; content of 144–145; incentives for 146–149; preferred delivery method 146–**147**, 153; protected continuous professional development 139–142; SEND Leader Integrated Model (SLIM) 153–154; time allocation for 143–144; visual connectivity schema of SENCO career trajectory 157
co-ordinating 110
core values, articulating 121–122, **127**
CPD *see* continuous professional development
critical thinking skills 94–96; analysis 99–100; questioning 97–98; reasoning 98–99; self-audit grid 101–103; synthesis 100–101
cumulative errors 123

decision-making *see* strategic decision-making skills
delivery and execution 18
disability **78**; specialist knowledge 74–76
duties of SENCO 8–10

Education Health and Care Plan (EHCP) 72–73, 123
EFA *see* exploratory factor analysis (EFA)
effective communication 87–88, **91**
effective leaders 70

# INDEX

effective pedagogical practice 70, **77**
EHCA *see* Education Health and Care Plan
EHCP 123
emotional capital 130–131
empathetic leadership 42
enablers 47
endurance 133, **136**
Equality Act 2010 75
ethos (ethical arguments) 17
evaluating options and solutions 122–124, **128**
expectations for SENCOs 20–21
expertise 18–19
exploratory factor analysis (EFA) 31

feedback 107

great teaching, factors that determine 23–24

human capital 131
human development 71–73

'I am' statements 63–64
identity 23–25, 46, 48, 52, 70; anchoring identity whilst doing the job 40–45; research design 5; themes of 64–65; transition from teacher to SENCO 36
identity work 24, 47, 68
incentives for continuous professional development (CPD) 146–149
inclusion 27, **78**; specialist knowledge 74–76
induction programme 79–80; NASENCO 36
induction qualification 33, 139
influence 46, 53; on leadership 108; leveraging 47–49
in-house promotions 32
interest factors for SENCO applications **32**
interpersonal skills 105–109; active listening 109–110; motivating self and others 112–114; self-audit grid 114–116; stretching colleagues 112; supporting teams 111
interview questions 25–27
inward-facing factors 31–32

job description (JD) 15
joy of learning 3

knowledge 18–19

leaders 81
leadership 17, 38–39, 43, 68, 81; connected leadership 67, 82, 95, 109, 130; effective leaders 70; empathetic leadership 42; influences 108; MAT leadership 108; professional curiosity 82; SENCO **12**, **15**, 16–18; Senior Leadership Team (SLT) 55–57,
59; transformational leadership 66–67, 82, 130
leadership formation 106–108
leadership skills 81; conflict management 88–89; effective communication 87–88; problem-solving 85–86; self-audit grid 90–92; team management 89–90
legislation: child development and needs 74; Regulation 50 (Children and Families Act, 2014) 4, 8–10; SEND Code of Practice 95–96
leveraging influence 47–49
line managing SENCOs 59–60
linear trajectory, transitioning teachers to SENCOs 33–34
listening 19; active listening 109–110, **115**
logos (logical disposition) 17

management: line managing SENCOs 59–60; SENCO **12**, **15**, 18–20; time management 132–133, **135**
mandatory training 50; *see also* training
marginalised role of SENCO 50
MAT leadership 108
MAT SEND 125
maturation and metamorphosis process 25–27
maturity 55
meetings, leadership skills 88
mentoring 43
metamorphosis approach, transitioning teachers to SENCOs 34–35
mission statements 119; *see also* vision
mixed messages 122
motivation 19, 100, 112–114, **116**

NASENCO; *see* National SENCO Award
National Professional Qualification (NPQ) SENCO 4, 25, 79–80
National SENCO Award (NASENCO) 4, 25, 32, 79–80; impact of 36
need 72
negotiation 46
no-choice factor 32
NPQ SENCO *see* National Professional Qualifications SENCO

one-off training sessions 138
one-page profile person-centred tool 82–83
online SENCO forum 146
outward-facing factors 31–32, 53

paradoxes 49
pathos (emotional buy-in) 17
pay progression for SENCOs 146–148
PD *see* professional development

peacekeepers 125
peacemakers 125
peer-to-peer mentoring model 43
peer-to-peer capital support 53
people pleasers 47
perseverance 133
person description (PS) 15
person-centred approaches 25
persuasion 46–47
persuasiveness 134, **136**
persuasion 17
power 46
preferred delivery method, for continuous professional development 146, **147**, 153
preparation 18
presentations, leadership skills 88
Prevent Strategy and British Values curriculum 25
primary need 72
private shadows 49
problem-solving, leadership skills 85–86, **91**
productivity 132
professional boredom 123–124
professional curiosity 82
professional development (PD) 18, 138
professional skills 130–131; endurance 133, **136**; persuasiveness 134, **136**; self-audit grid 134–137; self-management 131, **135**; time management 132–133, **135**
profile person-centred tool 82–83
protected continuous professional development 139–142
provision management 96
PS *see* person description

QTS *see* qualified teacher status
qualifications 37, 79–80
qualified teacher status (QTS) 4, 25, 32
questioning, critical thinking skills 97–98, **102**
questions for interviews 25–27

reasonable adjustment (RA) 75
reasoning, critical thinking skills 98–99, **102**
reasons for becoming SENCOs 31–32
recruiting SENCOs 22–29; applying for SENCO role **38**; in-house promotions 32
reductionism 12
reflection 107
reflective practice 28
reflexive 107
Regulation 50 (Children and Families Act, 2014) 4, 8–10
relational connections 19
relationship boundaries, setting 124–126, **128**
research design 4–6
responsibility 24; for SEND 83–85

rest 132
retention of SENCOs 51–52
review for growth 18
role of SENCOs 11–14
RUFDATA (reason, use, focus, data, audience, timescale and agency) 4

safeguarding 2
scaffolding in education 111
scaffolding theory 72
SCM evaluation approach 4
secondary need 72
self-audit grid: critical thinking skills 101–103; interpersonal skills 114–116; leadership skills 90–92; professional skills 134–137; specialist knowledge 76–79; strategic decision-making skills 126–128
self-directed continuous professional development (CPD) 142
self-management 131, **135**
self-perception 64
self-talk 64, 134
SEN *see* special educational needs
SENCO JD 15
SENCO Regulations Act 3–4
SENCO systems 44–45
SENCO trajectory **39**; stages of **60**
SEND *see* special educational needs and disability
SEND expertise 69
SEND Leader Integrated Model (SLIM) 15, 20–21, 65–66, 79–80, 151–154
SEND MAT Central Team 108
SEND Reforms in England 2014 67, 105
SEND Support 19
SEND7 9, 22, 37, 75, 90, 134
SEND8 134
Senior Leadership Team (SLT) 55–57, 59, 108
setting direction 43–44
simplicity the 'other' side of complexity, role of SENCO 13
simplicity this side of complexity, role of SENCO 12
SLIM *see* SEND Leader Integrated Model
SLT *see* Senior Leadership Team
social capital 53, 131
social justice 24; conceptual framework 51; person-centred approaches 25
solutions, evaluating 122–124, **128**
special educational needs (SEN) 73–74, **78**
special educational needs and disability (SEND) 3; responsibility for 83–85
specialist knowledge 64, 67–69; child and young person development 71–73; disability and inclusion 74–76; effective pedagogical practice 70; self-audit grid 76–79; SEND

Leader Integrated Model (SLIM) 79–80; special educational needs (SEN) 73–74
spiral framework 51
spiral model of growth for the SENCO leader 51
spiral model that contributes to identity and growth 52
stages of SENCO trajectory **39**, **60**
status, leadership 56
status building 68, 105
staying the course 44
strategic decision-making skills 118; articulating and living out core values 121–122; defining a vision 118–121; evaluating options and solutions 122–124; self-audit grid 126–128; setting relationship boundaries 124–126
stretching colleagues 112, **116**
support for SENCOs 138
supporting teams 111, **115**
SWOT analysis (strengths, weaknesses, opportunities, threats) 124
synthesis, critical thinking skills 100–101, **103**

teachable 107
teachers: identity 23; reasons for becoming SENCOs 20, 31–32; training 139, 141; transitioning to SENCOs, 22–29, 31, 33–39
team building 19, 50
team management, leadership skills 89–90, **92**
TeamADL 120
teams 105; supporting 111, **115**
tensions 49

themes of: identity 64–65; Regulation 50 (Children and Families Act, 2014) 23–24
thought leadership 40
time allocation for continuous professional development (CPD) 143–144
time management 132–133, **135**
tips for SENCOs 42
TL *see* transformational leadership
to-do lists 44
training 139, 141; mandatory training 50; one-off training sessions 138; *see also* continuous professional development
transformational leadership (TL) 66–67, 79, 82, 130; *see also* leadership
transition from teacher to SENCO 22–29, 31; exceptional cases 35–39; linear trajectory 33–34; metamorphosis approach 34–35
trust 17
trust triad 48

verbal communication 87
vision: articulating 17; communicating 17; defining 16, 118–121, **127**; writing 120
visual connectivity schema of SENCO career trajectory 157

wellbeing 41–43
whole school setting, leadership 16–17
work identity integrity violation/conflict 38
writing a vision 120
written communication 87

zones of proximal development (ZPD) 72

For Product Safety Concerns and Information please contact our EU representative  GPSR@taylorandfrancis.com
Taylor & Francis Verlag GmbH, Kaufingerstraße 24, 80331 München, Germany

www.ingramcontent.com/pod-product-compliance
Lightning Source LLC
Chambersburg PA
CBHW081946230426
43669CB00019B/2939